BASIC ENGLISH REVISION

T G Ledgard

Headmaster, Atherstone School, Warwickshire

and

C J S Garner

Director, Underwood College, Bournemouth

Cassell · London

Cassell Ltd
35 Red Lion Square, London WC1R 4SG
and at Sydney, Auckland, Toronto, Johannesburg,

an affiliate of Macmillan Publishing Co. Inc.,
New York

First published 1981

ISBN 0 304 30777 7

Printed and bound in Great Britain by
Morrison & Gibb Ltd, London and Edinburgh

INTRODUCTION

Level

This book has been written for the student who has completed several years of secondary education but who still has certain difficulties with written English. It is suitable, therefore, for any of the following:

* those studying on a GCE or CSE course
* students in Further Education on BEC or TEC courses
* anyone undergoing training, especially in the secretarial and business world
* people wishing to improve their written English for personal or professional reasons.

Contents

The book covers all the essential elements of written English. It is divided into five self-contained parts with the main emphasis on spelling and punctuation. A third part deals with the common errors most often found in written English and there are two further sections on handwriting and layout. These five subjects are covered comprehensively with explanations, examples and exercises on each point discussed. The book ends with a short section explaining the small number of technical terms used and a final part giving answers to all the exercises.

How to use the book

The book may either be followed as an integrated course from start to finish or, if you have difficulty with certain specific elements of written English, you may study only those parts or units which you need. The student following the whole course should spend as much time as is necessary on each individual item in the book before going on to the next point. Exercises and tests provide a constant means of monitoring progress. Wherever possible, the book should be studied with a teacher who can answer questions, provide further testing, adapt material for specific purposes, insist on accurate checking and so on. Where a teacher is not available, the book may be followed on a self-study basis. This will produce good results as long as the exercises are done conscientiously and the answers checked meticulously.

WINDSOR & MAIDENHEAD COLLEGE
GENERAL STUDIES DEPARTMENT

Thirty-nine.

This book (No. 39...) has been issued to the student named below, who is responsible for it, and for its replacement if it is lost or damaged.

Signature of Student	Course	Issued	Returned
Tona Bennett	Eng lang	26/9/89	3/10/89

CONTENTS

SPELLING

This part of the book consists of four sections, each dealing with a particular area of spelling difficulty, eg word endings. These sections cover all the main spelling problems that you are likely to have. Each section is sub-divided into units on specific examples, eg -able / ible endings, with explanations and exercises.

Explanations will be found, together with examples, on the left-hand page. Go through this page carefully, making sure you understand everything that is said. Study the examples given. Before turning to the exercises, test yourself — or get someone to test you — so that you are absolutely sure of all the rules, explanations and examples. Then do the **exercises.** These are on the opposite page and should be completed as follows:

(i) Write out the answers in full on a sheet of paper (preferably in a book or file).

(ii) When doing the exercises, do not look back at the previous page of explanation.

(iii) When you have finished all the exercises, check your answers carefully with the answers given at the end of the book. If possible, ask someone to do the checking for you since it is often difficult to see your own mistakes.

(iv) Write out corrections for all mistakes. It is a good idea to have a separate booklet for these corrections; you can also use it to write down difficult new words or any words which you frequently misspell. Test yourself regularly on these words.

When writing out corrections, follow this method: write out the word correctly three times, cover the word up, write the word again, check your answer.

In addition to the explanations and exercises, each section begins with a checking exercise and ends with a section test.

The **checking exercise** checks your ability to see and hear small differences. This is important since many spelling errors are the result of careless attention to detail.

The **section test** finds out how well you have remembered the explanations and exercises of the particular section. The fact that you spell a word correctly today is no guarantee in itself that you will spell it correctly the next time. Constant practice and repetition are necessary.

7

Section I: Sight and sound

Same sounds

Checking exercise IA

This is the first of your checking exercises. On the opposite page you will find two diagrams of a parking meter. At first glance these diagrams seem to be identical, but there are a number of small differences between them. Look carefully at both the labelling and the drawing of each diagram and see how many differences you can spot. You should be able to find twelve differences in all.

Make a brief note of each difference (other than position of lettering) you find and then turn to page 137 in the ANSWERS to check whether you are right.

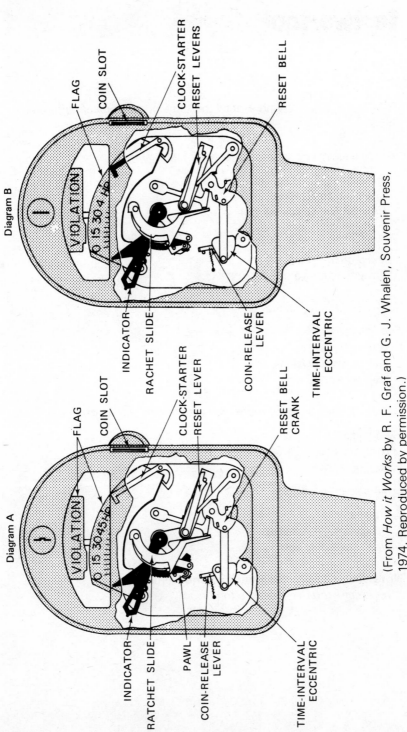

Diagram B

Diagram A

FLAG
COIN SLOT
CLOCK-STARTER RESET LEVERS
RESET BELL
VIOLATION
0 15 30 45

INDICATOR
RACHET SLIDE
COIN-RELEASE LEVER
TIME-INTERVAL ECCENTRIC

FLAG
COIN SLOT
CLOCK-STARTER RESET LEVER
RESET BELL CRANK
VIOLATION
0 15 30 45

INDICATOR
RATCHET SLIDE
PAWL
COIN-RELEASE LEVER
TIME-INTERVAL ECCENTRIC

(From *How it Works* by R. F. Graf and G. J. Whalen, Souvenir Press, 1974. Reproduced by permission.)

to/two/too

These three words sound exactly the same but they mean different things.

A. *to* usually tells you the direction of something.

Examples:
>   *She goes **to** College.*
>   *How far is it **to** the centre?*

You also write:

>   *It is a quarter **to** five.*
>   *Are you ready **to** go?*

B. *two* is the number *2* .

Examples:
>   **two** *coffees*
>   *twenty-***two** *players*
>   **two**-*way street*

C. *too* means either (i) *more than usual* or *more than expected.*

Examples:
>   **too** *much rain*
>   **too** *expensive*

or (ii) *also* or *in addition.*

Examples:
>   *He speaks Chinese **too**.*
>   *Her sister came **too**.*

Note: The following are written as **one** word:
>   *together   today   tonight   tomorrow*

Exercise 1: Put *to* or *too* in the following spaces.

(a) I'm off .... Spain this summer. Would you like .... come ....?
(b) Do I have ....? I'd rather go .... Greece.
(c) What about going .... Italy?
(d) Yes, I'd like .... do that.
(e) We might go .... Switzerland .... .

Exercise 2: From the following definitions find a word which begins *two-....* .

(a) having two colours
(b) made of two layers or strands, eg wood or wool
(c) piston which makes two movements for every explosion
(d) having two separate parts, eg a suit
(e) deceitful, insincere

Exercise 3: Put *to, two* or *too* into the following blanks.

(a) Far .... expensive.
(b) She thinks so .... .
(c) He's eighty-.... ....morrow.
(d) Tea for .... .
(e) .... fast for safety.
(f) Not .... well.
(g) Put .... and ....gether.
(h) .... be or not .... be.
(i) .... young .... marry.
(j) He's got .... cars. I'd like .... have .... , ...

your/you're; whose/who's

These pairs frequently cause confusion. If you follow the rules below, you should have no difficulty with them.

A. *your/you're*
your means *belonging to* or *relating to you*; it is always followed by a noun (see EXPLANATION OF TERMS, page 136.)

you're is short for *you are* (see APOSTROPHE, page 90); it is never followed directly by a noun.

Examples:
   your *mistake* but **you're** *wrong (***you are*** wrong)*
   your *stupidity* but **you're** *stupid (***you are*** stupid)*

yours is not exactly the same sound but it can cause difficulty. *yours* never has an apostrophe. You never write *your's*.

B. *whose/who's*
whose means *of whom* or *of which*.
who's is short for *who is* or *who has*.

Examples:
         My friend **who's** *over there (***who is*** over there)*
but   *The student* **whose** *book is missing*
         The boy **who's** *just had his birthday (***who has*** just had his birthday)*
but   *The boy* **whose** *birthday was yesterday.*

Exercise 4: Put *your* or *you're* in the following blanks.

(a) It's .... birthday; .... eighteen today
(b) I like .... jokes; .... joking
(c) .... tidy; .... tidiness
(d) .... mistaken; .... mistake
(e) .... go; .... going
(f) .... brilliant; .... brilliance

Exercise 5: Put *your, you're* or *yours* in these spaces.

(a) It's all .... fault
(b) .... sincerely
(c) .... on .... own now
(d) Is that watch ....?
(e) Is that .... record .... playing?
(f) It must be ....

Exercise 6: Put *whose* or *who's* in the following blanks.

(a) .... idea is that?
(b) .... done the work?
(c) .... at the door?
(d) I don't know .... it is
(e) The boy .... bike I borrowed
(f) The girl .... just started work

Exercise 7: The following words have different meanings depending on whether you put *your* or *you're* in front of them. Write out two phrases to show the difference in each pair.

Example: *right*   (i) *your right arm*
                    (ii) *you're right this time*

(a) cold
(b) kind
(c) flat
(d) left
(e) back

their/they're/there

These three words all sound exactly the same but they have very different meanings.

A.   *their* means *of, or belonging to, them*.

Examples:
   *What do you think of **their** new car?*
   *It's all **their** fault.*

Note: *theirs* is used when the noun following *their* is left out; it never has an apostrophe.

Examples:
   *What do you think of **theirs**? (What do you think of their house?)*
   *It's all **theirs**. (It's all their money.)*

B.   *they're* is short for *they are*.

Examples:
   They're *off*! (**They are** *off*!)
   *What do you think **they're** doing? (What do they think **they are** doing?)*

C.   *there* means *in, at or to a certain place or point*. It often means the opposite of *here*. Notice that the two words have a similar spelling.

Example:
   *You travel **here** and **there**, (but: You **hear** with your **ear**.)*

Note: *there's* is short for *there is*.

Exercise 8: Put *their, they're* or *there* into the following spaces.

(a) here and .... ; .... in here; here are .... papers
(b) near .... ; near .... home; .... near the pub
(c) in .... case; in .... ; .... in trouble
(d) over .... ; over .... dead bodies; .... over the worst
(e) .... you are; you're .... friend; it's you .... after

Exercise 9: Put *their, they're* or *there* into these spaces.

(a) .... off
(b) .... grandsons
(c) .... it is
(d) .... back

(e) nearly ....
(f) that's .... fault
(g) Who's ....?
(h) .... , ...

Exercise 10: Put *theirs* or *there's* into these blanks.

(a) It must be .... .
(b) .... no such thing.
(c) .... is the most difficult choice.
(d) .... a fly in my soup.
(e) Most people think .... is the best.
(f) Do you think .... a chance of winning?

Exercise 11: Put *their, they're, there, theirs* or *there's* into the spaces.

(a) I don't know what .... doing.
(b) .... a strange man standing over .... .
(c) I can't agree with you .... .
(d) They must all bring .... own lunch.
(e) While .... life, ... hope.
(f) .... over .... , playing with .... friends.

Same-sounding words

Exercise 12: Place the correct missing letter in each of the following blanks. What other word could be made up by the addition of a different letter?

Example:
The answers for *The car needed min..r repairs* would be (i) *minor — correct*; (ii) *miner — other word.*

(a) What's the curr..nt price of gold?
(b) Trafalgar was a famous nav..l battle.
(c) A six-b..rth sailing boat
(d) An eagle is a bird of pr..y.
(e) Of co..rse I like you.
(f) A du..l carriageway.

Exercise 13: Choose the correct alternative in each of the following. What does the other spelling of the word mean?

(a) I paid by check/cheque.
(b) The bride walked down the aisle/isle.
(c) He works on a building sight/site.
(d) All the fun of the fair/fare.
(e) The driver had to brake/break suddenly.
(f) Wear/where are you going?
(g) There is no write/right of way.

and for these:

(h) War and piece/peace	(n) A TV serial/cereal
(i) For sale/sail	(o) Good weather/whether
(j) Royal mail/male	(p) Full board/bored
(k) A lead/led pencil	(q) The idol/idle rich
(l) A prison sell/cell	(r) An oil magnet/magnate
(m) Iron ore/oar	(s) Good-buy/-by/-bye

Exercise 14: Find another way of spelling each of the words below without changing the sound. Make sure that you know the meaning of both words in the pair.

(a) made	(f) fowl
(b) hole	(g) waste
(c) new	(h) bury
(d) flower	(i) plain
(e) bare	(j) bowled

Similar sounds

Checking exercise IB

(i) Do the following pairs have the same or a different sound?

(a) to/two	(g) lose/loose	(m) recent/resent
(b) their/there	(h) write/right	(n) advice/advise
(c) hear/here	(i) clothes/cloths	(o) practice/practise
(d) we're/wear	(j) sight/site	(p) sell/cell
(e) you're/your	(k) board/bored	(q) race/raise
(f) off/of	(l) quiet/quite	(r) serial/cereal

(ii) Which of the following words rhyme with the word *slow*?

(a) how	(g) owe	(m) tough
(b) low	(h) hoe	(n) though
(c) mow	(i) shoe	(o) through
(d) now	(j) sew	(p) rough
(e) tow	(k) allow	(q) dough
(f) vow	(l) depot	(r) enough

(iii) For each word in column **A** find a word in column **B** which rhymes with it.

A	**B**
(a) peace	(h) goose
(b) ace	(i) geese
(c) juice	(j) source
(d) yes	(k) nurse
(e) worse	(l) fuss
(f) horse	(m) plaice
(g) plus	(n) chess

(iv) This is an exercise to be done aloud. The following words can be pronounced in two different ways. For each word give both pronunciations and both meanings.

(a) row	(e) read
(b) bow	(f) lead
(c) sow	(g) bass
(d) tear	(h) invalid

off/of/'ve

These three words are often confused. Remember that *off* and *of* are pronounced differently, and *of* usually sounds the same as *'ve*.

A. *off* has the general meaning of *away from* or *down from*.

Example:
  He fell **off** *his bike.*

It can also have a number of different meanings.

Examples:
  The strike is **off** *(cancelled).*
  This milk is a bit **off** *(sour).*

B. *of* usually joins two nouns.

Examples:
  a sheet **of** *paper*
  the Isle **of** *Wight*
  loss **of** *appetite*

C. *'ve* is the short form of *have*. The apostrophe shows that the first two letters (*ha*) are missing.

Examples:
  They **'ve** *gone.* (*They* **have** *gone.*)
  We **'ve** *seen it.* (*We* **have** *seen it.*)

Exercise 15: Put *off, of* or *'ve* into the following blanks.

(a) The cup .... tea fell .... the table.
(b) The meeting .... the social committee was called .... .
(c) We .... just broken .... our engagement.
(d) Though not well .... , he was highly thought .... .
(e) They live just .... the main road .... the town.
(f)   I .... no idea what became .... him.

Exercise 16: Write out correctly any of the following which are wrong.

(a) Are the brakes off?
(b) A jar've honey
(c) Top of the Pops
(d) The player was of side
(e) I could of seen him
(f)   Keep of the grass
(g) She should've gone

Exercise 17: Each of the following sentences has two meanings. Explain the difference.

(a) It's an island $\frac{of}{off}$ England.

(b) She took 10% $\frac{of}{off}$ the price.

(c) We're going $\frac{of}{off}$ course.

(d) He was speaking $\frac{of}{off}$ the record.

(e) Take the top $\frac{of}{off}$ the saucepan.

Exercise 18: Think of a word beginning with *off* to fit the following definitions. Some of them have hyphens.

(a) child or children
(b) casual manner
(c) cream or pale grey
(d) during less busy times
(e) shop selling alcohol
(f)   away from the mainland
(g) method of printing

Similar-sounding words

Exercise 19: Say each pair of words aloud and then write down the correct one.

(a) A living room suit/suite
(b) At a lose/loose end
(c) They adopted/adapted a child
(d) She was formally/formerly dressed
(e) Machine parts are made on a lath/lathe
(f) In his best cloths/clothes
(g) A resent/recent article in the paper
(h) What do you want for dessert/desert?
(i) Nobody's prefect/perfect
(j) I except/accept what you say
(k) The country/county of Lancashire

Exercise 20: Put each word in the following pairs into the appropriate space.

(a) *quiet/quite* — That will be .... all right as long as they are .... .
(b) *expect/except* — I .... to see her every day .... Sunday.
(c) *breath/breathe* — It's difficult to .... when you're out of .... .
(d) *later/latter* — The .... example comes .... in the book.
(e) *insured/assured* — He .... me that his bike was .... .
(f) *through/thorough* — She made a .... search .... her suitcase.

Exercise 21: Explain the difference between each word in the following pairs.

(a) decent/descent
(b) personal/personnel
(c) access/excess
(d) corporation/cooperation
(e) flagrant/fragrant
(f) deceased/diseased
(g) respective/respectful

Instructions for section tests

At the end of each of the four sections in the Spelling part of this book there is a test for you to complete. If you have understood and remembered the spelling patterns of each section, you should be able to score 100% on this test.

Each test consists of twenty short phrases from which one word has been left out. You are given three possible ways of spelling this word (**A, B** or **C**), only one of which is correct. Write down the spelling and the letter which you think are correct. If you are in any doubt, put down the fourth letter, **D. Do not guess the answer.**

Take as much time as you need to do the test. The important thing is to get all the spellings right and for the right reasons. If necessary, think back to the rules and patterns that you have studied in the section being tested — but do not look back at any previous pages.

When you have finished the test, check your answers carefully, add up your score and then look at this assessment:

Score	Assessment
20	Excellent. Carry straight on with the next section.
19	Good. Why did you make this one mistake? Remember the correct spelling next time.
17 – 18	Look carefully at your mistakes before going on to the next section. Write out the corrected spellings.
16 or less	Too many errors. If your mistakes are bunched together, you are having difficulty with one particular pattern. Study this pattern again (or more than one if necessary) before going on to the next section. Write out the corrected spellings.

Sight and sound: section test I

	A	B	C	D
1. It's .... easy	to	two	too	
2. That makes	to	two	too	
3. Much .... much	to	two	too	
4. Me	to	two	too	
5. Is that ....?	your	you're	yours	
6. .... go	your	you're	yours	
7. .... going	your	you're	yours	
8. .... sincerely	your	you're	yours	
9. .... off!	their	they're	there	
10. Almost	their	they're	there	
11. It's .... turn	their	they're	there	
12. .... new car	their	they're	there	
13. The plane took	off	of	've	
14. You .... seen it	off	of	've	
15. The strike is	off	of	've	
16. They .... gone	off	of	've	
17. Iron	oar	ore	or	
18. .... of way	right	write	rite	
19. 5 .... 2 metres	buy	by	bye	
20. .... and sound	site	cite	sight	

Section II: Word-building

Checking Exercise II

Look at each of the following signs briefly, cover it up and then write down exactly what you have just read. When you have done all of them, check your answers very carefully indeed.

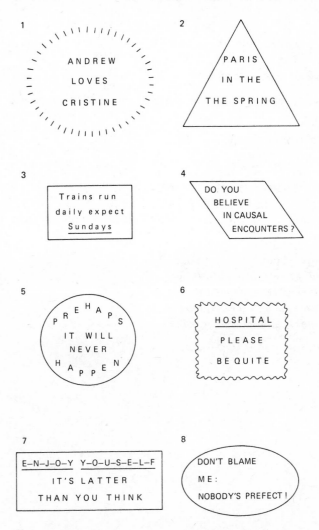

1

ANDREW
LOVES
CRISTINE

2

PARIS
IN THE
THE SPRING

3

Trains run
daily expect
Sundays

4

DO YOU
BELIEVE
IN CAUSAL
ENCOUNTERS ?

5

PREHAPS
IT WILL
NEVER
HAPPEN

6

HOSPITAL
PLEASE
BE QUITE

7

E–N–J–O–Y Y–O–U–S–E–L–F
IT'S LATTER
THAN YOU THINK

8

DON'T BLAME
ME :
NOBODY'S PREFECT !

Adding to final e

When a word ends in -e it sometimes loses the -e when a suffix (see
EXPLANATION OF TERMS, page 136) is added.

**When a suffix beginning with a vowel (see EXPLANATION OF
TERMS) is added, the final -e drops off**.

Examples:

*Lik**e** + **i**ng = liking*
*hop**e** + **i**ng = hoping*
*forgiv**e** + **a**ble = forgivable*

Note: The letter -y counts as a vowel when added as a suffix.
Therefore:

*simpl**e** + **y** = simply*
*eas**e** + **y** = easy*

There are a few exceptions to this rule, particularly when the endings
-ce or -ge are added to a suffix beginning with -a or -o. The final -e
stays in order to keep the sound soft. Here are all the common
examples:

*coura**ge** + **o**us = courageous*
*advanta**ge** + **o**us = advantageous*
*noti**ce** + **a**ble = noticeable*
*chan**ge** + **a**ble = changeable*
*mana**ge** + **a**ble = manageable*

Exercise 22: Add the suffixes below and spell the complete word in each case.

(a) amuse + ing =   (f) argue + able =   (k) courage + ous =
(b) write + ing =   (g) value + able =   (l) arrive + al =
(c) breathe + ing = (h) love + able =   (m) survive + al =
(d) hope + ing =   (i) advise + able =   (n) notice + ably =
(e) use + ing =   (j) change + able =   (o) translate + or =

Exercise 23: Turn the following nouns into adjectives (see EXPLANATION OF TERMS, page 136) by adding the letter -y. Sometimes you will have to double the final consonant (see EXPLANATION OF TERMS).

(a) shine   (e) sun   (i) craze
(b) haze   (f) sand   (j) mud
(c) fog   (g) fun   (k) ice
(d) noise   (h) breeze   (l) shade

Exercise 24: Turn the following verbs (see EXPLANATION OF TERMS) into negative commands.

Example:
  shout — no shouting
(a) smoke   (e) race
(b) overtake   (f) trespass
(c) dance   (g) skate
(d) shout   (h) cycle

Exercise 25: The two prefixes, *for-* and *fore-*, sound the same, but *fore-* has the meaning of *before in time* or *before in place*. Which of the following take *fore-* and which begin *for-*?

(a) head   (e) ground   (i) give
(b) get   (f) bid   (j) tune
(c) sight   (g) word   (k) man
(d) cast   (h) warn   (l) father

When adding a suffix beginning with a consonant, you do not drop the final -e.

Examples:
   like + **l***y* = *likely*
   use + **l***ess* = *useless*
   hope + **f***ul* = *hopeful*
   manage + **m***ent* = *management*

Apart from a few words ending in -*ly* (see page 28), the only exceptions to this rule are:

   awe + *ful* = *awful*
   argue + *ment* = *argument*

and a few numbers:
   nine + *th* = *ninth*
   five + *ty/th/teen* = *fifty/fifth/fifteen*
   twelve + *th* = *twelfth*

Note: Some words have alternative spellings. We can write the following with or without -*e*-:

   ageing or *aging*
   sizeable or *sizable*
   nosey or *nosy*
   judgement or *judgment*
   acknowledgement or *acknowledgment*

Exercise 26: Add the suffixes -*ment* and -*ing* to each of the following:

(a) arrange
(b) advertise
(c) develop
(d) excite
(e) argue

(f) achieve
(g) settle
(h) manage
(i) govern
(j) encourage

Exercise 27: Which of the following are incorrectly spelled? Write out the correct spelling.

(a) arguing
(b) developement
(c) judgment
(d) aweful
(e) ageing

(f) noticeable
(g) breatheing
(h) shadey
(i) arguement
(j) noisy

Exercise 28: Write out the following numbers in full.

Examples:
  £20.10 becomes *twenty pounds ten pence*
  1821 becomes *eighteen twenty-one*
  3rd March becomes *third of March*

(a) £19.50
(b) £90.15
(c) £40.14
(d) £4.90

(e) 1984
(f) 1564
(g) 1939
(h) 1415

(i) 5th October
(j) 9th August
(k) 12th July
(l) 19th May

Exercise 29: What is the difference in meaning in each of the following pairs?

(a) ore/or
(b) morale/moral
(c) humane/human
(d) bye/by

(e) heroine/heroin
(f) caste/cast
(g) urbane/urban
(h) loathe/loath

Adding -ly

To change an adjective into an adverb (see EXPLANATION OF TERMS, page 136), you normally add the suffix -ly.

Examples:
This is an **immediate** *problem*. becomes *Act* **immediately**.
She is a **careful** *worker*. becomes *She works* **carefully**.

When adding the -ly suffix, you do not change the base word.

Examples:
extreme + ly = extremely
sincere + ly = sincerely
incidental + ly = incidentally

There are three kinds of exceptions to the above rule:

A.   In these words the final -e disappears:

due + ly = duly
true + ly = truly
whole + ly = wholly

B.   Words ending in -y will change that letter to an -i- before the -ly suffix.

Examples:
happy + ly = happily
noisy + ly = noisily

C.   Words ending in -le just change the final -e to -y.

Examples:
simple + ly = simply
possible + ly = possibly
probable + ly = probably

Exercise 30:   Add -*ly* to the following words:

(a) hopeful
(b) general
(c) angry
(d) incidental
(e) childish

(f) heavy
(g) financial
(h) real
(i) suitable
(j) successful

(k) complete
(l) sensible
(m) scarce
(n) necessary
(o) physical

Exercise 31:   Spell correctly any of these words which are incorrect:

(a) usually
(b) immediatly
(c) especially
(d) extremely
(e) fortunatly

(f) approximately
(g) personally
(h) occasionaly
(i) absolutely
(j) accidentally

(k) defintley
(l) reliably
(m) busyly
(n) totaly
(o) duly

Exercise 32:   Business letters (see page 131) end as follows:

Yours (. . . .)

J Wilson

(Note that the *Y* of *Yours* is always a capital letter; the first letter of the next word is a small letter.)

(i) Turn the following into adverbs.

(a) sincere = Yours ....
(b) faithful = Yours ....
(c) cordial = Yours ....
(d) true = Yours ....

(ii) Which ending, *Yours sincerely* or *Yours faithfully*, goes with the following openings?

(a) Dear Sir
(b) Dear Mrs Thompson
(c) Dear Madam
(d) Dear John
(e) Dear Mr Hope

Adding -ful

Instead of writing:
> *The situation was* **full of hope**.

you can put:
> *It was a* **hopeful** *situation*.

Notice that the final *-l* of *full* disappears when it is added to a word.

Examples:
> *Lucy works with* **care**. can become *She is a* **careful** *worker*.
> *Last year was one of* **success**. can become *It was a* **successful** *year*.
> *Glass bottles create* **waste**. can become *They are* **wasteful**.

The rule, therefore, is
You do not change the base word when adding the suffix *-ful*.

Note: Remember to change the final *-y* to an *-i-* when adding *-ful*.

Examples:
> *full of duty* = *dutiful*
> *full of beauty* = *beautiful*

The only exceptions to the above rule are:
> *full of skill* = *ski**l**ful*
> *full of will* = *wi**l**ful*
> *full of awe* = *a**w**ful*

Exercise 33:   Add the suffix *-ful* to the following:

(a) peace
(b) care
(c) skill
(d) beauty
(e) doubt

(f) thank
(g) will
(h) use
(i) success
(j) awe

(k) pain
(l) plenty
(m) hope
(n) tact
(o) pity

Exercise 34:   The suffix *-less* usually makes a word negative. Write down all the words in the exercise above which can be turned into opposites by changing the *-ful* to *-less*.

Exercise 35:   Find a word ending in *-ful* to fit the following descriptions of people. The first letter is given in each case.

A person who

(a) is happy, lively   is c............
(b) doesn't remember things   is f............
(c) is considerate, thinks of others   is t............
(d) is shy, modest   is b............
(e) shows off, brags   is b............
(f) feels bitter, offended   is r............
(g) is stubborn, obstinate   is w............
(h) shows initiative, ability   is r...........
(i) shows lack of respect   is d............

Which adjective ending in *-ful* best describes you?

Prefixes

In this section we have seen how a word may change when a suffix is added. For example, *approve* + *ing* = *approving*; the *-e-* disappears.

When a prefix (see EXPLANATION OF TERMS, page 136) is added to a word, however, we do not alter the spelling.

dis + *approve* = *disapprove*
dis + *count* = *discount*
dis + *qualify* = *disqualify*

This gives us the following rule for prefixes:

You do not change the spelling of a word when adding a prefix to it.

This rule applies even when the last letter of the prefix is the same as the first letter of the word it is joining. You keep both letters.

Examples:

*di***s** + **s**atisfy = *di***ss**atisfy
*di***s** + **s**olve = *di***ss**olve

Exercise 36:   The following words can take the prefix *dis-* or *mis-*.
Choose the correct prefix and spell the complete word.

(a) solve
(b) spell
(c) satisfaction
(d) similar
(e) statement
(f) service
(g) solution
(h) shapen

Exercise 37:   (i) Write down the prefix in each of the following words
and explain what it means:

(a) nonsense
(b) submarine
(c) international
(d) extraordinary
(e) postscript
(f) bicycle
(g) maladjusted
(h) preview
(i) multicoloured
(j) television

(ii) Find one other word beginning with each of the above prefixes.

Exercise 38:   Here are three root words:

-port	with the general meaning of *to carry*
-pel	with the general meaning of *to drive*
-tract	with the general meaning of *to pull*

How many of the three root words can you add to each of the prefixes
below? Make sure that you know the meaning in each case.

(a) re.....
(b) de.....
(c) ex.....
(d) im.....
(e) dis.....
(f) pro.....
(g) com.....
(h) trans.....

Negative prefixes

A prefix is often added to give the opposite meaning to a word. All the following prefixes have the general meaning of *opposite of* or *not*. Notice that the prefix rule (do not change the spelling of a word when adding a prefix) still applies.

Prefix	Examples
dis-	*disadvantage*
	dissimilar
il-	*illegal*
	illiterate
im-	*impossible*
	immovable
in-	*incorrect*
	innumerable
ir-	*irregular*
	irrelevant
un-	*unkind*
	unnecessary

Exercise 39:   Make the following words into their opposites by adding a prefix from the list on the previous page.

(a) responsible
(b) mature
(c) rational
(d) mobile

(e) logical
(f) similar
(g) legible
(h) necessary

(i) modest
(j) literate
(k) satisfy
(l) relevant

Exercise 40:   Find a word which fits each of the following definitions. Each word begins with a negative prefix.

(a) against the law
(b) cannot be moved
(c) against nature
(d) beyond repair

(e) cannot be replaced
(f) cannot be resisted
(g) against the moral code
(h) cannot be reversed

Exercise 41:   Give each of these words an opposite meaning by changing the prefix:

(a) absent
(b) foreground
(c) exclude
(d) overrate
(e) polygamy

(f) pre-war
(g) benevolent
(h) dissuade
(i) dissociate
(j) dissent

Exercise 42:   Explain the difference in meaning between each word in the following pairs:

(a) immoral/immortal
(b) imminent/eminent
(c) immigrate/emigrate
(d) implicit/explicit

Word-building: section test II

For instructions on how to complete this test, see page 21.

		A	B	C	D
1	He's .... a report	writeing	writting	writing	
2	A .... person	foregiving	forgiveing	forgiving	
3	A .... place	shady	shadey	shaddy	
4	Industrial	developement	development	developpment	
5	A heated	argument	arguement	arggument	
6	A flower	arrangment	arangement	arrangement	
7	.... difficult	extremly	extreemly	extremely	
8	Come	immediately	immediatly	immediatley	
9	Yours	sincerly	sincerely	sincerley	
10	.... on time	usualy	usally	usually	
11	He .... believes me	realy	reely	really	
12	A .... great man	truly	truely	truley	
13	She drinks	noisly	noisily	noisely	
14	A .... sign	hopefull	hopeful	hopful	
15	A .... businessman	successful	succesful	successfull	
16	A .... morning	beautifull	beautiful	beautyful	
17	A .... worker	skillful	skilful	skilfull	
18	An .... pattern	iregular	irreguler	irregular	
19	.... parking	ilegal	illegul	illegal	
20	A .... customer	disatisfied	disatissfied	dissatisfied	

Count your score and look at your assessment on page 21.

Section III: Endings

Checking exercise III

Compare the two columns very carefully and decide for each number whether **A** is exactly the same as **B**. For each number write S if the columns are the same and D if they are different.

	A	**B**
1	accessory	accessory
2	antimony	antinomy
3	centimetre	centimeter
4	conscience	conscience
5	expensive	expansive
6	immunisation	immunisation
7	indelible	inedible
8	ordinance	ordnance
9	prescription	proscription
10	sulphide	sulphite

Do the same for the following:

11	Mrs J. H. Ridley	Mrs J. H. Ridley
12	3819-1916-318	3819-1619-318
13	if it isn't in it	if it isn't if it
14	Order No. PZ 8955	Order No. PZ 8955
15	What did she say	What did she say?
16	£19,685.33	£19,685.33
17	Tel: 0202 22624	Tel 0202 22624
18	He couldn't tell which of them he liked most.	He couldn't tell which of of them he liked most.
19	Grosvenor House Trelawney Street	Grosvenor House Trelawmey Street
20	84456983115	84456983115
21	&* – %;?:!	&* – %;?;!
22	Flight BA 78-690	Flight BA 78-690

able/ible

These two suffixes always sound the same. Although there are no absolute rules to tell you when to write -*ible* and when -*able*, you should find the patterns below useful.

Words ending -*able* **can often be divided into separate words that make sense.**

Examples:
  able to accept = acceptable
  able to adapt = adaptable
  able to depend on = dependable

Words ending -*ible* cannot usually be divided in this way. You cannot separate *visible* and *possible* into words that make sense.

Note: Words ending in -*e* usually drop this letter when adding -*able*.

Examples:
  value + able = valuable
  desire + able = desirable

Most words with -*s* **or** -*ss* **before this suffix take the** -*ible* **ending.**

Examples:

*respon***sible**	*permi***ssible**
*fea***sible**	*acce***ssible**
*sen***sible**	*po***ssible**

Exercise 43:   Write *a* or *i* in the following blanks:

(a) poss..ble
(b) accept..ble
(c) profit..ble
(d) compar..ble
(e) respons..ble

(f) depend..ble
(g) desir..ble
(h) prob..ble
(i) vis..ble
(j) comprehens..ble

(k) imagin..ble
(l) cred..ble
(m) access..ble
(n) avoid..ble
(o) agree..ble

Exercise 44:   Add a prefix to each of the words in Exercise 43 to make them into opposites.

Exercise 45:   Complete the following by adding *a* or *i* and then match each letter to its appropriate number:

(a) indel..ble
(b) illeg..ble
(c) ined..ble
(d) inelig..ble
(e) intellig..ble

(i)   poor handwriting
(ii)   clear explanation
(iii) bad stain
(iv) overweight bachelor
(v)   wet sandwiches

Exercise 46:   Write down each of the words below and after each write the number of one of the items from the list which follows:

(a) inconsiderable
(b) indispensable
(c) inflammable

(d) impracticable
(e) incompatible
(f) invaluable

List of items

(i) £100
(ii) roses
(iii) Crown Jewels
(iv) underwater football
(v) oxygen

(vi) fish and chips
(vii) nail polish
(viii) Concorde
(ix) ½p
(x) chalk and cheese

ant/ent

You will usually find that the endings *-ant* and *-ent* are used for adjectives while *-ance* and *-ence* are noun endings.

Examples:

Adjectives	Nouns
An import**ant** man	The import**ance** of man
A relev**ant** question	The relev**ance** of a question
A differ**ent** opinion	A differ**ence** of opinion
A confid**ent** youth	The confid**ence** of youth

Although there are no rules to tell you when to put *-ant* or *-ent*, and *-ance* or *-ence*, remember that the letter *-a-* or *-e-* always stays in different forms of the same word.

Examples:

Always letter *-a-*	**Always letter** *-e-*
import**a**nt	differ**e**nt
import**a**ntly	differ**e**ntly
import**a**nce	indiffer**e**nt
unimport**a**nce	differ**e**ntial

Exercise 47: Put the letter *a* or *e* into the blanks.

(a) abs..nt
(b) dist..nt
(c) import..nt
(d) reluct..nt

(e) rec..nt
(f) perman..nt
(g) innoc..nt
(h) relev..nt

(i) compet..nt
(j) adjac..nt
(k) compon..nt
(l) extravag..nt

Exercise 48: Do the same with the following:

(a) refer..nce
(b) confer..nce
(c) allow..nce
(d) sent..nce
(e) influ..nce

(f) perform..nce
(g) prefer..nce
(h) conveni..nce
(i) independ..nce
(j) toler..nce

Exercise 49: Make nouns out of the following verbs, eg *persist* becomes *persistence*. The last four words need special care.

(a) differ
(b) endure
(c) exist
(d) appear

(e) assure
(f) insure
(g) disturb
(h) reside

(i) enter
(j) offend
(k) pretend
(l) maintain

Exercise 50: Make adjectives out of the following verbs, eg *persist* becomes *persistent*. The words in the right-hand column need special care.

(a) confide
(b) ignore
(c) insist
(d) resist
(e) observe
(f) please

(g) obey
(h) abound
(i) suffice
(j) dominate
(k) excel
(l) appear

ar/er/or

These endings are often used for **people**, eg *teach**er**, decorat**or**, burgl**ar***. The columns below give you most of the words that cause spelling problems. Not many words end *-ar*. As a general rule, choose *-or* if you are in doubt between an *-er* and *-or* ending.

-**or**	-**er**	-**ar**
director	*adviser*	*registrar*
inventor	*barrister*	*scholar*
negotiator	*designer*	*vicar*
operator	*lecturer*	
solicitor	*organiser*	
supervisor		

Most **adjectives** take the *-ar* ending.

Examples:

circular	*peculiar*	*regular*
familiar	*popular*	*similar*

Many items of **equipment,** etc take *-or*.

Examples:

calculator	*duplicator*	*motor*
projector	*razor*	*tractor*
transistor	*word-processor*	

Note the exception: *computer*

Exercise 51:   Add -ar, -er, or -or to the following:

(a) doct..

(b) operat..

(c) prison..

(d) direct..

(e) burgl..

(f) profess..

(g) spons..

(h) negotiat..

(i) solicit..

(j) barrist..

Exercise 52:   What are the people called who do the following?

(a) invent

(b) design

(c) organise

(d) survey

(e) inspect

(f) decorate

(g) edit

(h) translate

(i) commute

(j) conduct

(k) supervise

(l) advise

Exercise 53:   Write out correctly any of the following which are wrong:

(a) duplicator

(b) computor

(c) familar

(d) reguler

(e) peculiar

(f) grammer

(g) processor

(h) calculater

(i) similur

(j) popular

(k) particuler

(l) projector

Exercise 54:   Make adjectives from the nouns in brackets.

(a) (circle) a ...... saw

(b) (nucleus) a ...... explosion

(c) (muscle) a ...... contraction

(d) (spectacle) a ...... fall

(e) (rectangle) a ...... shape

and from these:

(f) (sun) ...... energy

(g) (moon) ...... module

(h) (stars) ...... dust

ary/ery/ory; al/el/le

-ary/ery/ory

These endings are difficult to spell because we usually pronounce them in the same way, [ri], without the first vowel sound. We write *mystery* but we say [mistri]. You will need to learn these words in their groups.

-ary	**-ery**	**-ory**
elementary	*cemetery*	*compulsory*
library	*jewellery*	*factory*
ordinary	*mystery*	*laboratory*
preliminary		*satisfactory*
secretary		
temporary		

-al/el/le

These endings are also difficult because they are also usually pronounced in the same way, [ul]. We write *little* but we say [litul]. Here are the most common examples.

-al	**-el**	**-le**
casual	*channel*	*angle*
identical	*libel*	*article*
practical	*model*	*bicycle*
technical	*novel*	*people*
typical	*quarrel*	*vehicle*

Note: For *principal/principle* and *stationary/stationery*, see page 62.

Exercise 55: Add -al, -el or -le to the following:

(a) litt..
(b) quarr..
(c) peop..
(d) technic..
(e) vehic..

(f) casu..
(g) identic..
(h) hand..
(i) medic..
(j) ank..

(k) visu..
(l) jung..
(m) annu..
(n) physic..

Exercise 56: Add -ary, -ery or -ory to the following:

(a) libr...
(b) myst...
(c) fact...
(d) ordin...
(e) compuls...
(f) cemet...
(g) tempor...
(h) secret...

(i) prim...
(j) mem...
(k) snobb...
(l) summ...
(m) annivers...
(n) honor...
(o) confection...
(p) access...

Exercise 57: Make adjectives from these parts of the body. Each one ends in -al and the first letter is given in each case.

(a) mouth   o......
(b) mind   m......
(c) tooth   d......
(d) hand   m......
(e) voice   v......
(f) back   d......

Exercise 58: Match the following beginnings and endings to make complete words.

(a) mob...   -al
(b) mod...   -ul
(c) mog...   -yl
(d) met...   -ile
(e) mett...   -el
(f) meth...   -le
(g) menth...   -ol

Adding s (plurals)

As you know, most nouns add an -s to make them plural, eg *one team* but *two teams, a girl* but *five girls.*
This general rule has a few variations:

A.   Words ending with a hissing sound (*-s, -ss, -sh, -z, -x, -ch*) make their plural by adding *-es*.

Examples:
bus	*buses*
glass	*glasses*
bush	*bushes*
bench	*benches*

B.   Words ending *-f* and *-fe* almost always change to *-ves*.

Examples:
loaf	*loaves*
knife	*knives*

C.   Words ending *-y* change to *-ies* if the letter before the final *-y* is a consonant.
    If the letter before the final *-y* is a vowel, they simply add *-s*.

Examples:
*sto**ry***	*sto**ries***	but	*stor**ey***	*stor**eys***
*ene**my***	*ene**mies***	but	*conv**oy***	*conv**oys***
*compa**ny***	*compa**nies***	but	*holid**ay***	*holid**ays***

Note: This rule also applies when *-s* is added for other reasons.

Examples:
fly	*he flies*
play	*she plays*

Exercise 59:   Write out the plural of the following:

(a) box
(b) dress
(c) wife
(d) church

(e) tax
(f) thief
(g) self
(h) dish

(i) knife
(j) six
(k) wish
(l) watch

Exercise 60:   Make the following singular:

(a) lives
(b) addresses
(c) shelves
(d) authorities
(e) exercises

(f) inquiries
(g) sentries
(h) ladies
(i) halves
(j) businesses

Exercise 61:   Write out the plural of the following:

(a) party
(b) monkey
(c) apology
(d) berry

(e) butterfly
(f) opportunity
(g) secretary
(h) jersey

(i) difficulty
(j) factory
(k) valley
(l) lorry

Exercise 62:   Write out the correct form of any of these plurals which are wrong:

(a) chimnies
(b) handkerchiefs
(c) countries
(d) journies
(e) branches

(f) anniversarys
(g) cliffs
(h) skys
(i) loafs
(j) ministries

Irregular plurals

A. Words ending in -o add either -s or -es to make them plural. The most common words taking -es are:

tomato — *tomatoes*   *potato* — *potatoes*   *hero* — *heroes*
echo — *echoes*   *Negro* — *Negroes*   *veto* — *vetoes*

B. Some words have an irregular plural.

Examples:

child	*children*
woman	*women*
tooth	*teeth*
mouse	*mice*
man	*men*

C. Not all words ending in -s are plural.

Examples:
The news **is** *bad.*   NOT   *The news are bad.*

D. You must **never** add an apostrophe to make a word plural.

Examples:

Singular	**Plural**	**NEVER**
one day	*seven days*	*seven day's*
a coffee	*three coffees*	*three coffee's*
an apple	*four apples*	*four apple's*
a team	*two teams*	*two team's*

Exercise 63:   Add -*s* or -*es* to the following words to make them plural.

(a) radio	(e) piano
(b) potato	(f) tomato
(c) photo	(g) solo
(d) hero	(h) veto

Exercise 64:   Write down the singular of the following plural nouns.

(a) women	(e) deer	(i) shoes
(b) teeth	(f) children	(j) echoes
(c) feet	(g) oxen	(k) toes
(d) geese	(h) sheep	(l) media

Exercise 65:   Which of these words are plural (and should be followed by *are*) and which are singular (and should be followed by *is*)?

(a) news	(e) economics
(b) artists	(f) scissors
(c) series	(g) crisis
(d) politics	(h) athletics

Exercise 66:   Write down any of the following words which do not normally have a plural form.

(a) direction	(f) government
(b) information	(g) furniture
(c) sugar	(h) signature
(d) cigar	(i) address
(e) equipment	(j) progress

Endings: section test III

For instructions on how to complete this test see page 21.

		A	B	C	D
1	An .... person	adaptible	adaptabul	adaptable	
2	Who's ....?	responsable	responsibl	responsible	
3	An .... occasion	agreable	aggreable	agreeable	
4	A .... necklace	valuable	valueable	valuble	
5	A .... colour	different	diferent	diffrent	
6	She's often	absant	abscent	absent	
7	Whenever it's	conveniant	convenient	convienent	
8	Car	maintainence	maintenance	maintenence	
9	He's a	superviser	supervisor	supervizer	
10	That's a .... idea	pecular	peculier	peculiar	
11	.... studies	computor	computer	computar	
12	A .... address	tempary	tempory	temporary	
13	The local	cemetry	cemetery	cemetary	
14	A .... person	practicle	prakticle	practical	
15	A motor	vehicle	vehicul	vehical	
16	Two	loaves	loafs	loafes	
17	Three ...	companys	company's	companies	
18	Several	addresses	addreses	address's	
19	.... of the past	echoes	echos	echo's	
20	Many	journies	journey's	journeys	

Count your score and look at your assessment on page 21.

Section IV: Helpful hints

Checking exercise IV
This exercise tests your powers of memory and observation.

A. Answer these questions without looking at any other part of the book.

1 In the two diagrams of the parking meter at the beginning of this book
   (a) how many differences were there between the two diagrams and how many of them can you remember?
   (b) what word appears on the flag of the meter to show that the time limit has expired?
   (c) where was the coin slot — right or left, top or bottom?
   (d) what was the interval between the numbers on the time scale — 5, 10, 15 or 30 minutes?

2 What word did you have to spell in the last question of the last section test?

3 Describe the cover of this book as fully as you can — title, colour, etc.

4 Who published this book and who wrote it?

B. Here are some questions with more individual answers.

5 What were your first words this morning?

6 What were you doing a year ago at this time?

7 What is your earliest childhood memory?

8 Describe how someone you saw yesterday was dressed.

9 What was the weather like a week ago today?

10 Without looking around the room where you are writing this,
   (a) describe the handle of the door
   (b) what colour is the ceiling?
   (c) how many panes of glass are there in the window nearest to you?
   (d) what is the floor made of?

ice/ise

Should you write *football practice* or *football practise*? This often causes difficulty. Here is the rule:

Write -c- when it is a noun.
Write -s- when it is a verb.

Examples:

I give you advice.
What is your advice? }   *advice* here is a noun and therefore
My lawyer's advice   written -ce.

I advise you
What do you advise? }   *advise* here is a verb and therefore
My lawyer advises   written -se.

Remember the difference in pronunciation between *advice* and *advise* and you will have no problems. You wouldn't say *I advice you* or *This is my advise,* so you must not write it that way either.

Practice and *practise* follow the same rule (although here the pronunciation is the same).

Examples:

Noun		Verb
golf practice	but	*I practise golf.*
shorthand practice	but	*She practises shorthand.*
daily practice	but	*We practise every day.*

Exercise 67: Put *c* or *s* into the following blanks.

(a) my doctor's advi..e; please advi..e me
(b) a driving licen..e; I'm licen..ed to drive
(c) practi..e more often; football practi..e
(d) he devi..ed a plan; a strange devi..e

Exercise 68: Which of the following are incorrect? Write them out correctly.

(a) weekly practice   (e) put into practise
(b) netball practise   (f) legal practice
(c) out of practise   (g) he practises medicine
(d) general practice   (h) practice makes perfect

Exercise 69: Put *c* or *s* into the following blanks.

(a) You should take legal advi..e.
(b) Her father advi..ed her not to marry.
(c) It was a devi..e for measuring speed.
(d) That idea will never work in practi..e.
(e) They devi..ed a scheme for making money.
(f) Does anyone have the gift of prophe..y?
(g) The students were left to their own devi..es.
(h) What would you advi..e me to do?
(i) Practi..e what you preach.
(j) He runs an off-licen..e
(k) Let me give you a piece of advi..e.
(l) I prophe..ied that war would break out.
(m) He has a licen..e to practi..e.

Doubling the consonant

When you add a suffix beginning with a vowel to a word which ends in a single consonant, you sometimes have to double the consonant. The rule is:

With words of one syllable you must double the final consonant when there is only one vowel letter before it.

Examples:

Final consonant after single vowel		Suffix beginning with a vowel		
run	+	-er	=	*runner*
get	+	-ing	=	*getting*
rob	+	-ed	=	*robbed*

If there are two vowel letters (or another consonant) before the final consonant, just add the suffix.

Examples:
groan + *ing* = *groaning*
fail + *ed* = *failed*
kill + *er* = *killer*

Note: Remember that words ending in *-e* often lose this letter when adding a suffix (eg *write* + *ing* = *writing*). See page 24.

Exercise 70:   Add the suffix *-ing* to the following words.

(a) beat	(g) win	(m) sleep
(b) hit	(h) mean	(n) hop
(c) treat	(i) run	(o) shop
(d) cut	(j) plan	(p) leap
(e) sit	(k) groan	(q) drop
(f) knit	(l) spin	(r) droop

Exercise 71:   Add the suffixes at the top of each column to the words below.

-ed	**-er**	**-age**
(a) drop	(f) rub	(k) break
(b) heat	(g) hit	(l) stop
(c) rob	(h) plan	(m) wreck
(d) plan	(i) read	(n) haul
(e) grit	(j) stop	(o) scrum

Exercise 72:   Complete this grid:

	hot	**hotter**	**hottest**
(a)	big	....	....
(b)	....	....	fittest
(c)	cool	....	....
(d)	....	wetter	....
(e)	dear	....	....
(f)	....	....	meanest
(g)	sad	....	....
(h)	....	taller	....

Be careful with the last two — they are irregular:

(i)	bad	....	....
(j)	....	better	....

ie/ei

The letters *ie* and *ei* are found in the middle of many words. How can you be sure which way round to write them? There are two rules and the first rule is:

i before e except after c
When the sound is *[ee]*

Examples are *shriek, piece* and *diesel* which all have the sound *[ee]* and therefore the *i* comes before the *e*.

Deceive, ceiling and *receive* have the sound [ee] but, since it comes after the letter *c*, you write the *e* before the *i*.

Exception: There are only two words which do not follow this rule. They are:

seize

protein

When the letters *ie* and *ei* do not make the sound [ee], there is another rule.

Put them round the other way
When the sound is *[ay]*.

Examples are *weigh, vein* and *neighbour,* which all have the sound [ay] and therefore the *e* comes before the i.

When you do not have the sound [ee] or [ay], some words will be written *ei*. Here are all the most common words:
foreign, height, leisure, weird, weir
A few words are written *ie*. Here they are:
view, fierce, pierce, sieve, friend

Exercise 73: All these words have the sound [ee] or [ay]. Put *ie* or *ei* into the blanks.

(a) bel...f
(b) f...ld
(c) conc...t
(d) th...f
(e) s...ze

(f) w...ght
(g) n...ghbour
(h) ...ght
(i) fr...ght
(j) v...n

(k) hyg...ne
(l) prot...n
(m) d...sel
(n) s...ge
(o) rec...pt

Exercise 74: Complete the following words with *ie* or *ei*.

(a) for...gn
(b) v...w
(c) fr...nd
(d) l...sure
(e) h...ght

(f) w...rd
(g) f...rce
(h) p...rce
(i) w...r
(j) s...ve

Exercise 75: The following verbs all have the sound [ee]. Write out correctly any which are spelled wrongly.

(a) perceive
(b) relieve
(c) beleive
(d) deceive

(e) grieve
(f) recieve
(g) acheive
(h) retrieve

Exercise 76: Make nouns out of each of the verbs in Exercise 75, eg *perceive* becomes *perception*.

Exercise 77: Find a word with either *ei* or *ie* in it which has the same sound as each of the following words, eg *sealing = ceiling*.

(a) peace
(b) seas
(c) ate
(d) way

(e) air
(f) rein
(g) vale
(h) vain

Silent letters

Silent letters at the beginning of words

English words are full of silent letters. These letters are never pronounced but they must always be written.

Here are some examples of silent letters, all of which come at the beginning of words.

Initial silent letter	When	Examples
g-	always before *n*	*gnome, gnat, gnaw, gnash*
h-	sometimes silent	*honest, hour, honour, heir*
k-	always before *n*	*knee, knock, knight, knowledge*
p-	always before *s* or *n*	*psychology, pseudo, psalm pneumonia, pneumatic*
w-	always before *r* and sometimes *h*	*write, wrap, wrist, wretched who, whole*

Exercise 78:   Add one of the following silent letters — *p-*, *g-* or *k-* — to complete each of these words.

(a) ..nat
(b) ..not
(c) ..naw
(d) ..now
(e) ..new

(f) ..night
(g) ..neumonia
(h) ..narled
(i) ..nuckle
(j) ..neumatic

Exercise 79:   Which of the following need the silent letter *w-* to make them correct? Write out the complete word in each case.

(a) rist
(b) risk
(c) rinkle
(d) rink

(e) reck
(f) rong
(g) ren
(h) rent

(i) restle
(j) restless
(k) rigging
(l) riggle

Exercise 80:   In normal conversation the following pairs sound the same. Use them in phrases or sentences to show the difference in meaning.

(a) whether/weather
(b) wheel/we'll
(c) where/wear
(d) which/witch
(e) whine/wine

Exercise 81:   Find another way of spelling the sounds made by each of these words.

(a) herd
(b) hair
(c) heir
(d) hole

(e) horse
(f) hour
(g) hail
(h) him

Exercise 82:   Say the following aloud.

(a) as happy as Harry
(b) hale and hearty
(c) an honest hero
(d) our happiest hour
(e) a horrible headache
(f) an honourable heir
(g) a hysterical hostess

Silent letters in the middle and at the end of words

Silent letters also come in the middle and at the end of words. Here are the most common examples.

Silent letter	When	Examples
b	after *m*	*comb, lamb, thumb, plumber*
	before *t*	*doubt, debt, subtle*
c	after *s*	*science, descent, crescent, discipline*
d	before *g*	*bridge, budget, dredge, lodge*
g	before *n*	*sign, campaign, foreign, align*
gh	end of word	*though, thorough, plough*
	before *t*	*thought, ought, sight*
i	middle of word	*marriage, business, parliament*
l	before *d*	*could, should, would*
	before *k*	*folk, yolk, walk, chalk*
n	after *m*	*autumn, solemn, column, damn*
t	after *s*	*listen, castle, fasten, postpone*

Exercise 83: The final letter of each of the following words is silent. Write out each word with the letter added.

(a) colum..

(b) thum..

(c) bom..

(d) condem..

(e) clim..

(f) hym..

(g) crum..

(h) dum..

Exercise 84: Fill in the missing silent letter in each of the words below.

(a) dou..t

(b) fo..k

(c) de..t

(d) desi..n

(e) cou..d

(f) campai..n

(g) pa..m

(h) rei..n

Exercise 85: Write out each of the following words, adding a *t* where necessary.

(a) ca..ch

(b) wa..ch

(c) wa..sh

(d) sti..ch

(e) whis..le

(f) Chris..mas

(g) ba..chelor

(h) commit..ee

(i) atta..ch

(j) mor..gage

Exercise 86: Write out each of the following words, adding a *c* where necessary.

(a) ex..use

(b) ex..ellent

(c) ex..ercise

(d) ex..itement

(e) ex..ist

(f) ex..ess

(g) a..quire

(h) abs..ence

(i) s..issors

(j) lus..ious

(k) obs..olete

(l) cons..ious

Exercise 87: Which consonant is silent in each of these words?

(a) subtle

(b) crescent

(c) Wednesday

(d) cupboard

(e) answer

(f) receipt

(g) environment

(h) rhyme

(i) government

(j) miscellaneous

Exercise 88: Each symbol stands for a silent letter (or letters). When you have worked out what each symbol represents, arrange the letters to make a five-letter word. What is the word?

bou*t	bus&ness	cha + k
beha + f	plou*	lia&son
pos/pone	ki/chen	fli*t

Some difficult words

Some words often cause spelling problems, especially when there are no rules to help you. One of the best ways to deal with these words is to have a trick for remembering the spelling. As long as it helps you to get the spelling correct, any system will do. Here are a few hints which you may find helpful.

A. *Stationary* or *stationery?*
*station**a**ry* means not moving like a p**a***rked car.*
*station**e**ry* means writing materials, like l**ett**e*rs,* **e**nve*lop**e**s.*
Remember: E for Envelope in *station**e**ry*

B. *Principle* or *principal?*
*princip**le*** means general law, truth, eg *I agree in principle.*
*princip**al*** means (i) most important, eg *the principal cities of Europe.*
or (ii) the head of a College, eg *the Principal of the training college.*
Remember — AL is the name of a man. Therefore the person is always *Princip**al.***

C. *Loose* or *lose?*
*l**oo**se* means not tight, eg *these shoes are too loose.*
*l**o**se* means to have something no longer, eg *I'll lose my temper.*
*Remember: l**o**se has l**o**st an **o***

D. *Independent*
A person of independent means leads a life of **ease** (or E's).
Remember: 3 E's in *independent*

E. *Definite* is the opposite of *infinite.* Both have *-ite* endings.
Or ..... *def**i**n**i**te* has two eyes (or **i**'s) and a nose (for **n**).

F. *Separate*
Remember: There's a *rat* in *sepa**rat**e.*

Consonant groups

It is sometimes difficult to know whether a word has a double consonant or not. Learn the following words in their groups.

Group 1 – single consonant only

until	*resort*	*pavilion*
procedure	*development*	*fulfil*
writing	*personal*	*enrolment*
altogether	*inoculate*	*instalment*

Group 2 – one double consonant

occasion	*error*	*opportunity*
necessary	*correspond*	*appropriate*
across	*personnel*	*vaccinate*
really	*parallel*	*symmetry*

Group 3 – two double consonants

possess	*committee*	*assassinate*
success	*accommodate*	*accessory*
assess	*embarrass*	*aggression*
address	*occurrence*	*commission*

Words to learn

Here is a list of words that often cause spelling difficulties. Make sure
that you know the spelling of each word.

anxious	humorous
beginning	initial
category	interrupt
certain	language
choice	luggage
colleague	medicine
college	negotiation
comparative	opinion
criticism	privilege
decision	pronunciation
desperate	recommend
disappointed	succeed
efficient	surprise
extension	technique
financial	undoubtedly

Helpful hints: section test IV

For instructions on how to complete this test, see page 21.

		A	**B**	**C**	**D**
1	Legal	practice	practise	practises	
2	He .... daily	practices	practise	practises	
3	Football	practice	practises	practise	
4	She .... it	droped	dropped	dropt	
5	I .... so	hoped	hopped	hopt	
6	Town	planeing	planing	planning	
7	Road	haullage	haulage	hauleage	
8	I .... you	belief	believe	beleive	
9	Next-door	neighbour	nieghbour	naybour	
10	A .... stamp	forign	foriegn	foreign	
11	Fine	wether	whether	weather	
12	I .... that	new	knew	nu	
13	Go	threw	thorough	through	
14	.... tables	separate	seperate	seprate	
15	That's	definite	definate	definit	
16	The College	Principle	Principal	Principel	
17	.... now	untill	un till	until	
18	Is it ....?	necessary	necesary	neccessary	
19	A great	ocasion	occasion	ocassion	
20	.... at last	sucess	succes	success	

Count your score and look at your assessment on page 21.

PUNCTUATION

Correct and systematic punctuation is as important as correct spelling. Bad punctuation can lead to confusion, eg

Can you come to a committee meeting on Tuesday we were given permission to use the committee room at the town hall.

This could mean either:

Can you come to a committee meeting on Tuesday? We were given permission to use the committee room at the town hall.

or

Can you come to a committee meeting? On Tuesday we were given permission to use the committee room at the town hall.

Not all poor punctuation will lead to such confusion but, if a reader cannot rely on your punctuation marks always being in the normal places and performing their normal functions, he will lose confidence in what he is reading and you will fail to convey your intended meaning fully, accurately and effectively.

In this part of the book there are units on all punctuation marks in all their usages, each containing explanations, examples and exercises. As with the Spelling part of the book, you may either go systematically through every unit or choose only those units which deal with your own particular difficulties.

Full stop

FULL STOP AT THE END OF A SENTENCE
Of all punctuation marks, the full stop at the end of a sentence is the most important. If you do not use it correctly, anything you write will be difficult to understand.

You must put a full stop (or question mark or exclamation mark) at the end of every sentence.

To put full stops in the right place, therefore, you have to know what a sentence is.

66

A sentence is a group of words which makes complete sense by itself.

For example, if you went up to someone and said *a dirty face* or *walking down the street*, they would not know what you meant. These groups of words have no complete meaning by themselves and so they are not sentences. But you could say *It's a nice day*. That group of words makes complete sense by itself and is therefore a sentence.

Remember also that each sentence must begin with a capital letter.

Exercise 89:   Some of the groups of words below are sentences (because they make complete sense by themselves). Write out only these groups of words. Remember that you must put a capital letter at the beginning and a full stop at the end of each sentence.

Example:
  the boat sank very quickly becomes *The boat sank very quickly.*

(a) you forgot to feed the tropical fish
(b) a mechanic who always kept his finger-nails clean
(c) if you aren't prepared to work really hard
(d) she danced with feeling and grace
(e) singing in the rain
(f) Edinburgh is the capital city of Scotland
(g) she slammed the food down in front of her husband
(h) good morning
(i) a dead dog, lying in the road
(j) the importance of writing correct English

Exercise 90:   Do as you did in Exercise 89.

(a) a beautiful sunset
(b) please sit down
(c) the ice was dangerously thin
(d) the disgusting habit of dropping litter
(e) annoyed by the loudness of the music being played in the next room
(f) a beautiful white swan, gliding smoothly down the river
(g) please don't cut too much off
(h) he wanted to be a surgeon but he couldn't stand the sight of blood
(i) note-taking is a very useful skill
(j) a long way from home and feeling very lonely

To say that a sentence is a group of words which makes complete sense by itself is not, however, quite enough. It works very well if all the sentences are simple ones. Sometimes, though, a sentence has several parts, for example:

The dog slept quietly in his basket while the burglar was stealing the money.

If we follow the rule we have used so far, we would put a full stop after *The dog slept.* These words make complete sense by themselves.

But, if we do this, we are left with the words, *quietly in his basket while the burglar was stealing the money.* These words do not make complete sense by themselves; they do not form a sentence and we cannot have parts of sentences left over. The only way we can make sense of these words is by adding them to the first group of words, *The dog slept.* This gives us a complete sentence:

The dog slept quietly in his basket while the burglar was stealing the money.

So we have to add something to our first definition of a sentence.

A sentence is a group of words which makes complete sense by itself, but it may be necessary to add other groups of words which cannot stand as sentences on their own.

Exercise 91:   Some of the groups of words below are one sentence; some are two or more. Write out each group, adding full stops and capital letters where they are needed.

Example:
  the small dog yapped at the visitor it snapped at his heels
becomes *The small dog yapped at the visitor. It snapped at his heels.*

(a) i like this programme it's eductional
(b) he was not very old but he was nearly bald
(c) it has rained all week the farmers are happy again
(d) you can't wear that dress, Mary it's far too tight it's not nice
(e) if you don't believe me, ask Ted you know he always tells the truth
(f) he turned over and yawned widely
(g) don't touch that wire you'll electrocute yourself
(h) they went into the club it was quiet and almost empty they turned round and came out into the dark streets again
(i) with all the noise that was going on around her she found it very hard to concentrate on her work
(j) i love him i shall marry him if he asks me

Exercise 92:   Write out the following, adding only full stops and capital letters. You should have nine sentences when you have finished.

Sarah had never been out with a boy before so this evening was the first time she wasn't sure whether she was looking forward to it or not she was certainly excited she stood in front of the sitting-room fire in her new dress and tried to talk sensibly to her mother as she waited nervously for Edmund she didn't have long to wait she soon heard his footsteps coming up the front path the door opened and in he came her heart sank he was wearing jeans and a dirty denim jacket.

FULL STOP AFTER ABBREVIATIONS

An abbreviation is a shortened word. Sometimes a word is shortened to one letter (the first) and sometimes to a few letters.

There used to be a rule that each abbreviated word was followed by a full stop.

Examples: *Mr.*   *B.B.C.*   *e.g.*

Although it is still correct to punctuate abbreviations in this way, it is now increasingly common (and acceptable) for abbreviations to be written without full stops.

Examples: *Mr*   *BBC*   *eg*

At present people vary in their use of the full stop after abbreviations; some people use it always, some use it sometimes and some never. It cannot be said, therefore, that there is a rule for you to follow.

However, certain practices do seem to be acceptable, and we recommend:

A.   For the printed word (typed or printed material):
No full stops at all after abbreviations.

Examples: *Mr P J Williams*   *pm*   *Ltd*   *EEC*

You will notice that we have followed this practice ourselves and left out full stops after all abbreviations in this book.

B.   For handwriting:
No full stops after abbreviations except after a person's initials.

Examples: *Mr P. J. Williams*   *pm*   *Ltd*   *EEC*

However you decide to punctuate abbreviations, **you must follow a consistent pattern.**

If you decide to follow the old rule and place a full stop after each abbreviated word, you should know that placing a full stop after an abbreviation makes no difference to any other punctuation. You can have a full stop followed by another punctuation mark, for example

A. C. Dunnit & Co. Ltd., 25 Commercial Rd., Winsborough.

A final note: according to the International System of Units, abbreviations of units of measurement, eg *cm (centimetre), kg (kilogram), km (kilometre)* or *ml (millilitre)*, **must not** be followed by a full stop. *p (pence)* also **must not** be followed by a full stop.

Question mark

A question mark at the end of a sentence shows that a question has been asked. The rule is:

If a sentence asks a question, you must place a question mark at the end. A question mark stands instead of a full stop and must be followed by a capital letter.

Example:
Did you pass your exam?

Exercise 93: Some of the sentences below are questions. They need a question mark at the end. The others are not and so need a full stop. Write out each sentence, adding the correct punctuation mark.

Examples:
What is that boy's name becomes *What is that boy's name?*
but *His name is James* becomes *His name is James.*

(a) Will you give me a ride on your motorbike
(b) You are earning less than you would get if you were out of work
(c) The Principal gave an impressive speech
(d) What is today's date
(e) Today is August 11th
(f) Why are you making so much noise
(g) I can't be bothered to work in the evenings
(h) Is it true that Ben and Alison have broken up
(i) Your library book is long overdue
(j) When does the disco start tonight

You have to be careful with some sentences which sound like questions but which are really not.

Robert asked what they were having for supper.

This may sound like a question but, if you think about it clearly, you will realise that it is a statement. It tells you what Robert said; it does not ask a question. You need a question mark only if you are writing down the actual question:

What are we having for supper?

Exercise 94:   Do as you did in Exercise 93. Work out carefully whether each sentence is a question or a statement.

Examples:
  I don't know who you are becomes *I don't know who you are.*
  but *Who are you* becomes *Who are you?*

(a) I know why she refuses to go out with you
(b) Why didn't you vote for me as student president
(c) She asked if she could try on the long cotton dress
(d) Why don't my parents leave me alone
(e) He had no idea why she would not talk to him
(f)   I don't understand how you can support the present Government
(g) Can you lend me some money, Bill
(h) Whether it's raining or not, I shall still go for a walk after dinner
(i)   Does John Travolta really have blue eyes
(j)   Why didn't you ask that policeman where the station is

Exclamation mark

An exclamation is a sharp expression, usually of strong feeling, often surprise. It may be one or two words or it may be a sentence. The rule is:

You must use an exclamation mark after an exclamation. An exclamation mark stands instead of a full stop and must be followed by a capital letter.

It is often up to you to decide whether to use an exclamation mark or a full stop — but, in general, do not use too many exclamation marks. Sentences like *I did enjoy that film.* are not really exclamations and should have only a full stop at the end.

These are the times when you **must** use an exclamation mark:

A.   Sentences (not questions) beginning with *What* or *How* are usually exclamations and so will end in an exclamation mark, eg *What a lovely day!* or *How pleased I am to meet you!*

B.   Short and sudden exclamations, standing by themselves, eg *Good Lord!* or *Stand back!* or *Oh!* or somebody's name — *Susan!* You can often, though, make these exclamations part of a sentence and so you will have a choice of punctuation, eg

Good Lord! It's raining! or *Good Lord, it's raining!*
and *Susan! Be quiet!* or *Susan, be quiet!*

(It is up to you whether you use an exclamation mark or a full stop after *raining* and *quiet*.)

Exercise 95:   Punctuate the following sentences correctly, adding only full stops, question marks and exclamation marks.

(a)   What a good tea that was
(b)   What are we having for tea
(c)   Let me out
(d)   Tibby Stop scratching the furniture
(e)   How unusual to meet a man who is interested in needlework
(f)   Dearest, I love you
(g)   Oh no He's dropped it
(h)   How are we going to climb that cliff
(i)   Mum Come here
(j)   Look out You'll knock over that old man

Capital letters for proper names (and inverted commas for titles)

Proper names begin with a capital letter.
Proper names are names of **particular** people, places, times and things (including titles of books, etc).

Examples: *Wendy, Scotland, Thursday, Ford*
Note that in titles of books, plays, films, television programmes, etc (**titles are always surrounded by inverted commas**) we do not begin an unimportant word like *the, a, to, it, from* with a capital letter unless it is the first word in the title, eg 'The Hunchback of Notre-Dame'.

Words formed from proper names nearly always begin with a capital letter, eg *German, Christian*.

Exercise 96: Write out the sentences below, adding capital letters for proper names and inverted commas around titles. Remember that the word *I* is always written as a capital letter and that sentences begin with a capital letter too.

(a) toby sinclair has lived in india for three years.
(b) one of britain's most popular television programmes was the forsyte saga.
(c) jane toogood and henry clark were married in st peter's church on saturday.
(d) he always spent his summer holiday looking at saxon churches.
(e) the italians are usually considered to be more emotional than the english.
(f) murder on the orient express was a film made from a novel by agatha christie.
(g) mrs williams took her old austin to the village garage.
(h) you will find the offices of j w brodie ltd at the end of market street.
(i) the royal air force suffered heavy losses during the battle of britain.
(j) i can't make up my mind whether i am a christian, an agnostic or an atheist.

Comma

The comma is used in a number of different ways, but always to separate words or groups of words from each other. It is not, however, as strong as a full stop, which is used to separate one sentence from another. It should **never** be used instead of a full stop.

The four sections which follow show the main uses of the comma.

THE COMMA PLACED BETWEEN ITEMS IN A LIST
A comma is placed between items in a list instead of *and* **or** *or*. The list may be of single words or groups of words.

Examples:

She put on lipstick, eye-shadow and mascara. (instead of *She put on lipstick and eye-shadow and mascara.*)

He frowned heavily, scratched his head, chewed his pencil and fidgeted in his chair. (instead of *He frowned heavily and scratched his head and chewed his pencil and fidgeted in his chair.*)

Would you prefer a vanilla, strawberry or chocolate ice-cream? (instead of *Would you prefer a vanilla or strawberry or chocolate ice-cream?*)

Exercise 97:   Place commas where necessary in the following sentences.

Example:

He ordered egg sausages beans tomatoes and chips. becomes *He ordered egg, sausages, beans, tomatoes and chips.*

(a) It would help the builders if they could have immediate delivery of the frames glass catches and hinges.
(b) It is just as important for a secretary to be clean neat punctual and polite as it is for her to be a good typist.
(c) She wondered whether he would prefer to go for a walk watch television read a book or just talk.
(d) Wilkie Stonehouse Dibley and Hazell were an effective goal-scoring combination.
(e) The fireman put out the flames quickly quietly and efficiently.
(f) The green plover peewit or lapwing can be identified by the round shape of its wings when in flight.

(g) He packed his toothbrush toothpaste and pyjamas and set off for the station.

(h) The night club was crowded smoky dark and noisy.

(i) She would not go out with any of them — Dave Jack Pete Harry or even Sylvester.

(j) He did not know whether to put on his brakes swerve violently or just go straight on and hope for the best.

A PAIR OF COMMAS to mark off describing groups of words which are not absolutely necessary

A sentence will often contain a describing group of words which should be marked off from the rest of the sentence. This is because the words are **not absolutely necessary** to the meaning; the sentence would still make good sense without them. To mark off such a group of words we use a pair of commas.

Pairs of commas are used round describing groups of words which must be marked off from the rest of the sentence because they are not absolutely necessary to the meaning.

There are three sorts of describing groups of words which, if they are not absolutely necessary, are marked off by commas:

A.   Groups of words which usually begin with a word ending in -*ing* or -*ed* and which come immediately before or after the person or thing they describe, eg:

The driver, shaking violently, bent over the man he had knocked down.

B.   Groups of words beginning with *who, which, whose,* etc and coming immediately after the person or thing they describe, eg:

The building, which was very tall, swayed with the wind.

C.   Groups of words (sometimes a single word) which are another way of naming the thing they describe and which come immediately after it, eg:

The butcher, Mr Cleaver, sold two lamb chops to Mrs Webb.

In all of the above examples the describing groups of words could be left out because they are **not absolutely necessary** to the meaning and the sentence would still make good sense without them.

Notice that, when a describing group of words which should be surrounded by a pair of commas begins a sentence, it does not need the first comma. In the same way, such a group of words at the end of a sentence has a full stop (or question mark or exclamation mark) instead of the second comma.

Examples:

Shaking violently, the driver bent over the man he had knocked down.

Mrs Webb bought two lamb chops from the butcher, Mr Cleaver.

Exercise 98: Each of the sentences below contains a describing group of words which is not absolutely necessary to the meaning of the sentence. Write out each sentence, adding commas where necessary.

Example:

The Prime Minister Mr Gresham offered his resignation to the Queen. becomes *The Prime Minister, Mr Gresham, offered his resignation to the Queen.*

(a) The tyres squealing as they went round the corner were beginning to show signs of wear.

(b) My grandfather a well-known citizen of the town had a street named after him.

(c) Sid Green who had done no work that morning was told off by the foreman.

(d) John made no attempt to speak to Carol who was sulking in front of the television.

(e) Shouting at the tops of their voices the crowd cheered the home team to victory.

(f) This morning I met Jack Banks of whom you spoke yesterday.

(g) The cat licked its fur singed by the sparks from the fire.

(h) The uneven wicket because of which many balls bounced viciously was responsible for the dismissal of the first four batsmen.

(i) The new stand recently built by the contractors was a great success.

(j) The Fastnet yacht race claimed several casualties mostly from the smaller boats.

We have learned that describing groups of words which are not absolutely necessary to the meaning of a sentence should be marked off with commas. It is, however, important to remember that, if any of the describing groups of words **is** absolutely necessary, then it must **not** be marked off with commas. For example, in the sentence:

The student who cheated in the exam was not given a certificate.
the describing group of words, *who cheated in the exam,* **is** absolutely necessary to the meaning of the sentence. Without it we should have
The student was not given a certificate.
which does not make the required sense, because we do not know which student is meant.

So we can say that, **if we do not know** who or what is meant without the describing group of words, then the group of words is absolutely necessary and should not be hidden away between a pair of commas. **If we do know** who or what is meant without the describing group of words – as we would if the sentence was *Sharon Lewis, who cheated in the exam, was not given a certificate.* – then the group of words is not absolutely necessary and should be marked off with commas.

Exercise 99:   Each of the sentences below contains one or more describing groups of words. Some are **not** absolutely necessary to the meaning of the sentence and should therefore be marked off with commas; others **are** necessary and should not be marked off with commas. Write out each sentence, adding commas where necessary.

Examples:
Mr Phillips smoking a pipe sat down in the armchair. becomes *Mr Phillips, smoking a pipe, sat down in the armchair.* but *The man smoking a pipe sat down in the armchair.* is written out exactly as it is.

(a) I loved the blouse which you were wearing yesterday.
(b) Sally saw Mr Chapman the manager of the supermarket for a preliminary interview.
(c) Eddy who had never fished before caught three mackerel off the rocks with a spinner.
(d) Holding each other closely as they danced they were oblivious of all around them.
(e) The man who is wearing the brown jacket is the man who tried to pick my pocket.
(f) She was pleased to give a pound to the charity for which the children were collecting.
(g) A large cheque was sent to Oxfam on behalf of which the concert had been put on.
(h) Gordon Lee's recent release 'Troubled' has wasted no time in getting to the top of the charts.
(i) They leaned over the rails and watched the horses parading round the paddock.

(j)   The programme 'Killer' which was on the television last night was very frightening.

COMMAS TO MARK OFF GROUPS OF WORDS beginning with *when, after,* **etc**

As a general rule, a comma is used after groups of words beginning with *when, after, before, until, while, since, if, unless, although, though, because* (and certain other words) if these groups of words **begin a sentence,** eg:

If people insist on large pay increases, the cost of living will rise rapidly.

A pair of commas is used around groups of words beginning with *when, after,* etc if they come **in the middle of a sentence,** eg:

The Chancellor says that, if people insist on large pay increases, the cost of living will rise rapidly.

No commas are necessary if the group of words comes **at the end of a sentence,** eg:

The cost of living will rise rapidly if people insist on large pay increases.

The rule, therefore, is

Groups of words beginning with *when, after,* **etc are marked off with commas when they come at the beginning or in the middle of a sentence.**

Exercise 100:   Each of the following sentences contains a group of words beginning with *when, after,* etc. Write out each sentence, adding commas where necessary. Some of the sentences will not need any commas.

Example:
If you smoke forty cigarettes a day you will ruin your health.
becomes *If you smoke forty cigarettes a day, you will ruin your health.*

(a)   Tom knew he would have to work really hard if he was going to pass his exams.
(b)   Although you have the qualities we need I am afraid we do not have a vacancy.
(c)   The family agreed that while Tessa was studying they would not have the radio on.
(d)   They agreed that they would not have the radio on while Tessa was studying.
(e)   The match will not be played unless the pitch dries out.

(f)   She said that because he had lied to her she could never trust him
      again.
(g)   When Bonzo was six months old his training began.
(h)   The English although they had a smaller army defeated the French
      because they were better armed.
(i)   After they had put the ferrets in the boys waited hopefully for
      rabbits to come out into the nets.
(j)   She was furious with Marcel because he had dyed her hair the
      wrong colour.

OTHER USES OF THE COMMA

To mark off a term of address

   To address someone is to call them by name. When you do this, the
name must be marked off from the rest of the sentence by a comma (or
pair of commas).

Examples:
   Dorothy, you're late.
   Get out of bed, son.
   I wonder, Mr Stevens, if you could help me.

Exercise 101:   Mark off the terms of address in the following
sentences by adding commas where necessary.

(a)   Good afternoon Mrs Arbuthnot.
(b)   Ladies and gentlemen this is a great occasion.
(c)   I must ask you Mr Wiggins to accept my resignation.
(d)   Get off my foot you fat lump.
(e)   Sarah will you lend me that record you bought last week?
(f)   If you do not move further up the beach Your Majesty I fear you
      will get your feet wet.
(g)   Platoon attention!
(h)   You rotten thing you've taken my queen.
(i)   The most important thing to remember Daisy is that the customer
      is always right.
(j)   Why did you steal that pig Tom?

Between *he said* **and direct speech**

A comma is used (unless it would replace a question mark or an exclamation mark — they remain as they are) to separate *he said / asked*, etc from the actual words spoken, whichever way round they are written. Notice that the comma always comes before the adjacent speech mark.

Examples:

"I cannot find the fault," he said.
The shop assistant asked, "Does it fit you, Madam?"
(See page 87 for a full explanation of direct speech.)

Exercise 102: Write out the following sentences, adding a comma (or question mark or exclamation mark) to separate the direct speech from the other words. Remember that the added comma (or other mark) should come before the adjacent speech mark.

(a) "My punctuation is improving" she said hopefully.
(b) He began briskly "Today we shall learn about cyclones and their effects."
(c) "Why won't you come out with me" he asked desperately.
(d) Swaying over the microphone, the DJ said smoothly "It's great to see you all this evening."
(e) "If you had shown some common sense, the accident would never have occurred" he said sternly.
(f) "Look out" yelled the foreman.
(g) Mary asked nervously "Is the meal all right?"
(h) "Help" the man in the hang-glider shouted down from above their heads.
(i) "I still haven't found a job" she said sadly.
(j) The zoo-keeper said "Move slowly or you'll frighten him."

To mark off certain linking words or groups of words

There are a few single words or very short groups of words which are used to make a link between sentences and which are usually marked off by commas. These are:

however   *of course* *by the way* *well*
without doubt *moreover*   *nevertheless*

These words usually need to be followed by a comma when they come at the beginning of a sentence, eg:

Well, I didn't know what to do.

If they come in the middle or at the end of a sentence, they are usually marked off with commas, but not always. It is up to you to decide whether you think you need a pause before and after the word or words concerned. For example, you could have either:

She was, without doubt, the prettiest girl in the room.
or
She was without doubt the prettiest girl in the room.

Exercise 103: Write out the following sentences, marking off the linking words or groups of words with commas where you think it is necessary.

(a) The rescuers however held out little hope of finding the men alive.
(b) Of course the vandals had to pay for repairing the damage.
(c) The vandals had of course to pay for repairing the damage.
(d) Well there was nothing we could do about it.
(e) It was moreover a particularly windy evening.
(f) We were pleased to see him nevertheless.
(g) By the way have you met Jane Simpson?
(h) You are without doubt the biggest liar I have ever met.
(i) However they did not play the music as loudly as we had feared.
(j) The ball meanwhile had gone out of play.

In addresses

A comma may be used at the end of each line when you are writing an address (the last line ends in a full stop), eg

Miss Rosemary Day,

3 Park Avenue,

Bath,

Avon.

Nowadays, however, it is becoming more common to leave out all punctuation in addresses, eg

Miss Rosemary Day

3 Park Avenue

Bath

Avon

It does not matter which method you use, so long as you always do the same thing.

If you are using the comma, it is customary for the address of the writer at the top of the letter and the address on the envelope to be set out with the beginning of each successive line nearer by a regular amount to the right-hand side of the paper, ie sloped. If you are leaving out the comma, addresses are usually set out with each line starting immediately underneath the one above, ie blocked. You can see the two different kinds of layout in the two examples above. (For a fuller explanation of how to set out letters, see LAYOUT on page 126.)

Important: see Note (ii) on page 84.

In dates

A comma or commas may be used when writing dates. It may be placed between the day of the week (*Friday*), the day of the month (*20th November*) and the year (*1981*), eg:

Friday, 20th November, 1981 or *20th November, 1981* or *Friday, 20th November*

However, as with addresses, it is becoming more common to leave out such commas (and, when you do so, it is usual to write the date without the *-th*, etc after the day of the month), ie:

Friday 20 November 1981

It does not matter which method you use, so long as you are consistent.

Important: see Note (ii) on page 84. See also LAYOUT on page 126.

Starting and ending letters

A comma may be used after *Dear--------*, eg *Dear Sir*, or *Dear Wendy*,

A comma may also be used after the final greeting, whether it is *Yours sincerely*, or *Yours faithfully*, or *With best wishes*, or *With love*,

Again, however, as with the punctuation of addresses and dates, it is becoming more common to leave out such commas. After all, the position of the first and final greetings makes their meaning and purpose clear so that any punctuation could be said to be unnecessary. It does not matter which method you use so long as you are consistent.

Important: see Note (ii) below. See also LAYOUT on page 126.

Notes

(i) According to the International System of Units (SI), a comma should no longer be used between groups of three numbers, ie it is now wrong to write *5,182* or *48,561,718*. You should write either *5182* or *48561718* or, to make the reading of numbers easier, you may group the numbers in threes with a space between each group, eg *5 182* or *48 561 718*.

(ii) You have seen that the use of the comma in addresses and dates and starting and ending letters is up to you, so long as you follow a consistent pattern. It cannot, therefore, be said that there is a rule nowadays, but we recommend:

A.   For the printed word (typed or printed material): **no commas.**

B.   For handwriting: **put in all the commas**.

These recommendations fit in with the two on page 70 about the use of full stops after abbreviations and it would be consistent and sensible to follow the same pattern — either A (for the printed word) or B (for handwriting) — in all cases.

Speech marks

Whenever you are writing the actual words spoken by someone, you must enclose them in a pair of speech marks. The rule is:

Speech marks enclose the actual words spoken.

When you use speech marks, there are three points you must remember:

A.   Speech marks are always used in pairs. The first one comes at the beginning of the actual words spoken and the second comes at the end, eg:

"I feel tired today."

B.   Only the actual words spoken may come between the pair of speech marks, eg:

"Good morning," he said.

is right, but

"Good morning, he said."

is wrong — because the words *he said* were not actually spoken and so should not be inside the speech marks.

C.   You will notice that, wherever you write a speech mark (except at the beginning of a sentence), there is always a punctuation mark. This is usually a full stop or a comma, though it can be a question mark or exclamation mark. The speech mark should always be placed just **after** the punctuation mark, eg:

"My head hurts," he said weakly.
Hopefully she asked, "Am I on the right bus for the station?"

Exercise 104: Place a pair of speech marks in each of the following sentences. Make sure that they enclose only the actual words spoken and that, wherever a speech mark is next to another punctuation mark, it is written just after that mark.

Example:

My tea is hot, complained Father. becomes *"My tea is hot,"* *complained Father.*

(a) I'm sorry, he apologised.
(b) Dan suggested, Let's stop at the next pub.
(c) Don't leave me! she sobbed.
(d) Why don't you look where you're going? demanded the old man as he struggled up from the pavement.
(e) I nearly caught it, said John as the fish wriggled off the hook and slipped back into the water.
(f) This election has been rigged! cried the losing candidate.
(g) Mrs Baker said sadly, My pot plants always die.
(h) I hope you're sorry for all the trouble you've caused, said the magistrate sternly.
(i) Two coffees, please, said Jenny.
(j) Sleepily she asked, What time is it?

The sentences in exercise 104 all contained words actually spoken. This is called **direct speech.** In the next exercise some of the sentences contain speech which is reported — **reported speech.** When speech is reported, we are not writing down the exact words actually spoken so we must **not** use speech marks, eg

Direct Speech   *"I am cold," he said.*
Reported Speech   *He said that he was cold.*

Exercise 105:   Do as you did in Exercise 104. In this exercise, however, three of the sentences are reported speech and should be written out exactly as they are — **without** adding speech marks.

(a) This pen always runs out of ink at the wrong time, muttered Charles to himself.
(b) The Prime Minister said that she would have no arguments in her Cabinet.
(c) The sergeant told his men, Don't shoot until you see the whites of their eyes!
(d) What is the name of this station? he asked, stretching himself and looking sleepily out of the carriage window.
(e) We've won! they shouted.
(f) Mrs Tappit asked her class how they expected to become typists without being able to spell correctly.
(g) He held the dead ferret in his hand and said sadly, I'll miss Fred — he was the best I've ever had.
(h) Can I borrow your hair-drier, please, Mum? asked Karen.
(i) You will kill yourself if you go on smoking, advised Dr Williams.
(j) Dr Williams told him that he would kill himself if he went on smoking.

Understanding where to place speech marks is, as you have seen, not difficult. Knowing how to use other punctuation marks when you are writing direct speech is equally straightforward.

A comma is used (unless it would replace a question mark or an exclamation mark) to separate *he said / asked,* etc from the actual words spoken, whichever way round they are written. This is explained on page 81, OTHER USES OF THE COMMA.

Except for this use of the comma, all the punctuation (including capital letters, small letters, question marks and exclamation marks) remains **exactly the same** as it would be if there had been no *he said*.

Look at this sentence:

Speech marks are easy to use.

If this was spoken by someone, you could write:

Mr Blenkinsop said, *"Speech marks are easy to use."*
or *"Speech marks are easy to use,"* said Mr Blenkinsop.
or *"Speech marks,"* said Mr Blenkinsop, *"are easy to use."*

Notice that the punctuation (in this case capital letters and full stop) remains exactly the same as in the original sentence except where a comma is used to separate *he said* from the actual words spoken. In the second example above, this means that the original full stop is replaced by a comma.

Question marks and exclamation marks, however, are never replaced by a comma, eg

"Do you understand speech marks now?" asked Mr Blenkinsop.
and *"You've forgotten to put in the speech marks again!"* exclaimed Mr Blenkinsop.
(Notice that in these instances, the question mark and exclamation mark are not followed by a capital letter as they normally would be.)

Exercise 106: Write out the following sentences and punctuate them correctly, using speech marks, capital letters, commas, full stops, question marks and exclamation marks where necessary:

(a) dinner will be served during the flight the air hostess told the passengers

(b) can you really concentrate on your work with the radio on so loudly Harry's mother asked

(c) nobody will give you a job said the careers officer unless you cut your nails and comb your hair

(d) he said firmly I'm not going to play cards with you again

(e) do you really think you look attractive asked Aunt Helen walking round with dirty jeans and holes in your tee-shirt
(f) these trousers are far too tight Mark told the sales assistant
(g) I'm very impressed said the manager and I should like to offer you the job
(h) eureka cried Archimedes
(i) you were unwise said Mrs Jenks to paint the walls blue and the ceiling orange
(j) Bonzo shouted his master come here at once

The last rule for writing direct speech is:

New speaker, new line.

This means that every time there is a change of speaker you must begin on a new line and in from the margin. You are, in fact, starting a new paragraph. Look at this example:

> *"Good evening, ladies and gentlemen," said the manager, moving towards the group of two men and two women who had just come into the restaurant.*
>
> *"Good evening," said the man in the dark suit. "Do you have a table for four?" The manager looked quickly round the dimly lit room.*
>
> *"Certainly, sir. Would you like to sit over there?"*
>
> *"Yes, that's fine," said the man. "Could we hang our coats up, please?"*
>
> *"I'll take them for you, sir."*

Exercise 107: Write out the following conversation, adding all the punctuation and starting each new speaker on a new line, in from the margin.

Hello said the boy who had just appeared in front of her hello said Penny he was obviously nervous so she smiled at him would you like a drink he asked no thanks she said would you like to sit down he sat down in the empty chair beside her and for a moment they looked in silence at the couples dancing in front of them have you come by yourself he asked Penny hesitated she didn't know whether to tell him that she had had an argument with Barry and that he'd gone off by himself no she said but I'm by myself now what about you I'm by myself he said my name's Stephen he hesitated then he looked at her and smiled for the first time shall we dance yes she said let's dance.

Note: Speech marks are also used around quotations. See LAYOUT, page 126, for an explanation of how to write quotations.

Apostrophe

The apostrophe shows that something has been left out, either the word *of* or a letter (or letters).

APOSTROPHE USED INSTEAD OF THE WORD *of*
There are two things you must know about the apostrophe used instead of the word *of*: when to use it, and exactly where to place it.

A.   When to use the apostrophe

A word ends in -'s or -s' to show that the order of the words has been changed and *of* **has been left out.**
In each of the examples below, the left-hand group of words is another way of saying the right-hand one; the order of the words has been changed and the phrase made shorter. In each case *of* has been left out, and so you have to write -'s or -s'.

My friend's house = The house of my friend
Jackie's book = The book of Jackie
The birds' nests = The nests of the birds
The babies' prams = The prams of the babies
The Women's Institute = The Institute of the Women

The same thing happens even with groups of words like

At the dentist's = At (the surgery of) the dentist
We are going round to Ted's = We are going round to (the house of) Ted
A month's holiday = A holiday of a month
Two weeks' pay = The pay of two weeks

In each case the order of the words has been changed and *of* has been left out.
You must beware, though, of adding an apostrophe to a word just because it ends in -*s*. This is a very common mistake. In the sentence, *The excited fans cheered the footballers,* the word order has not been changed and no *of* has been left out. The words ending in -*s* are merely plurals (more than one) and so there should be no apostrophe.

Exercise 108: Each of the twenty groups of words below contains one word ending in -'s or -s'. Ten of these are correct — because the original group of words has been shortened and *of* left out. The other ten are wrong — they are merely plurals and should have no apostrophe. Write out all the groups of words, leaving out the apostrophe where it is wrong but copying out the words and apostrophe as they are if it is correct.

Example:

The twinkling light's becomes *The twinkling lights* but *The horse's hooves* should be written out exactly as it is because it is correct.

(a) The train's whistle
(b) The pattering raindrop's
(c) The hitch-hikers' rucksacks
(d) A bunch of bananas'
(e) The rustling leaves'
(f) The rabbits' burrows
(g) The clouds' passing overhead
(h) The firemen's helmets
(i) Mary's little lamb
(j) The bustling crowd of shopper's
(k) The ladies' room
(l) At the doctor's
(m) The sandwiches' on the plate
(n) A day's illness
(o) The donkey's on the beach
(p) A bus-load of holiday-makers'
(q) The cheering spectator's
(r) The chimpanzees' tea-party
(s) For heaven's sake
(t) The rose bushes'

B.   Where to use the apostrophe

Write the apostrophe at the end of the *of*-word.

This sounds complicated but it is really very simple. Imagine that you are not sure where to place the apostrophe in the phrase, *My friends house.* To decide the right place —

    (i) Change and lengthen the group of words in your mind so that it contains *of* — you will get *the house of my friend.*

    (ii) Ask yourself — What is the *of*-word, ie the main word that comes after *of*? It is *friend.*

    (iii) Place the apostrophe at the end of the *of*-word — *friend's.*
So you end up with *My friend's house.*

Here is another example. You are uncertain about the right place for the apostrophe in *The birds nests.*

    (i) Change the phrase to include *of* — *The nests of the birds.*

    (ii) What is the *of*-word? It is *birds.*

    (iii) Place the apostrophe at the end of the *of*-word — *The birds' nests.*

Exercise 109: Write out each of the groups of words below, adding the apostrophe in the correct place. Remember — the apostrophe comes at the end of the *of*-word.

Example:

The babys rattle (which is a shorter way of saying *The rattle of the baby*) becomes *The baby's rattle.*

(a) The books cover
(b) The mens leader
(c) My brothers girl-friend
(d) The Hikers Association
(e) Journeys end
(f) The ladies netball team
(g) The ships crew
(h) A months notice
(i) The Transport and General Workers Union
(j) A smokers cough

Exercise 110: Write out each of the sentences below, adding apostrophes where necessary. Some of the sentences may not need any apostrophes at all.

Example:

The cats eyes shone in the darkness like two coals of fire. becomes *The cat's eyes shone in the darkness like two coals of fire.*

(a) 'The Times' has been one of the countrys leading newspapers for about two hundred years.
(b) Dicksons savage shot bounced dangerously out of the goalkeepers hand.
(c) 'Gardeners Question-Time' is one of the longest-running radio programmes.
(d) Heather and Fiona bought two pieces of cod and two bags of chips.
(e) The Womens Lib movement has a large number of supporters in this country, rather more in the towns and cities than in the villages.
(f) The students eyes were fixed firmly on Mr Metcalfe as he spoke sternly from the platform, nor did the Principals words fall on deaf ears.
(g) The clowns trousers were baggy and full of holes.
(h) The parables of Jesus have at times been misunderstood.
(i) Edinburgh, Scotlands capital, is one of the worlds beautiful cities.
(j) Bill Joness overalls were lost so he bought some new ones.

APOSTROPHE USED TO SHOW THAT YOU HAVE MISSED OUT A LETTER OR LETTERS

Instead of saying *I did not understand*, you would usually say *I didn't understand*. You are running together two words (*did* and *not*) and shortening the sound of what you say (*not* becomes *n't*).

When this is written, you must write the two words together, without a break between them, and leave out a letter. In place of the missing letter (or, in some cases, letters) you always write an apostrophe – *didn't*.

The rule, therefore, is:

The apostrophe shows the missing letter or letters.

Remember that it does **not** show the break between two words.

Words which are often run together are: *isn't, don't, can't, it's, he's, you're, I'm, I'll, he'd, she's, we'd, o'clock (of the clock)*.

There are three further small points to remember:

A.   In *shan't* letters are left out in two places – *sha(ll) n(o)t* – but there is only one apostrophe. It shows the missing *o* in *not*.

B.   *will not* is shortened in an odd way: *won't*.

C.   *it's (it is)* is quite normal but, to show the difference between them, *its (of it)* **has no apostrophe,** eg *The snake shed its skin*.
Remember: *it's = it is; its = of it*.

Exercise 111:   Write out the following sentences, adding apostrophes where necessary.

(a)   Ill see if theres any cake left in the tin.
(b)   We shant get there in time if you dont hurry.
(c)   The dog wont go outside if its raining.
(d)   Its not fair – youre cheating.
(e)   The lights gone out and I cant find the candles.
(f)   Lets go and see if Sallys home yet.
(g)   Its a nuisance but theres no use worrying about it now.
(h)   If hes not home by ten o clock, Ill lock the front door.
(i)   Youll be sorry for what youve done when your fathers finished with you.
(j)   Im afraid Ive dropped a mug and its lost its handle.

Semi-colon

A semi-colon separates two groups of words which are closely linked in meaning and which could both stand as sentences on their own.

Example:

There was water everywhere; it had rained all night.

These two groups of words are obviously closely linked in meaning because the second tells you the reason for the first.

Note that each could also stand as a sentence on its own. You could write:

There was water everywhere. It had rained all night.

If, however, you had written *There was water everywhere because it had rained all night,* you could **not** separate the two groups of words with a semi-colon since *because it had rained all night* cannot stand as a sentence on its own.

Exercise 112: Each of the sentences below needs a semi-colon, a comma or a full stop in the middle. Write out each sentence, adding whichever punctuation mark seems most correct. (There is no doubt when a comma should be used, but you have a certain amount of choice between a semi-colon and a full stop.)

Example:

He fell asleep he was very tired. becomes *He fell asleep; he was very tired.*

(a) Desmond and Diana thought the film was very bad they decided to leave.

(b) Sally rushed breathlessly into the office she was late for work again.

(c) The motor-cyclist lay on the road his right leg twisted at an impossible angle.

(d) The motor-cyclist lay on the road his right leg was twisted at an impossible angle.

(e) Father came in from the garden it was getting dark.

(f) The family were all watching the play on the television Dick suddenly leapt to his feet.

(g) Miss Wilkinson put on her coat it had started to rain.

(h) She lay in bed sleeping peacefully until late in the morning.

(i) Wendy was tall and had beautiful black hair her sister was short and fair.

(j) James lifted his eyes from his exam paper and looked out of the window on the other side of the road he could see children playing in the park.

Colon

The colon has a special and definite use.

The colon means that something is to follow, often a list.
Two examples will best show the use of the colon:

To make flapjacks you need these ingredients: golden syrup, margarine, brown sugar and oats.

These were the last words of Captain Oates: "I am going outside and I may be some time."

Exercise 113: Write out the following sentences, adding a colon in the correct place. Do not add any other punctuation.

(a) There were four things which old Mr Bassett disliked long hair, loud whistling, hands in pockets and mumbled speech.

(b) This was the rallying-cry of the French Revolution "Liberty, Equality, Fraternity."

(c) The walls of Jenny's bedroom were completely covered with a colourful collection of various things photos, pictures, posters, record jackets and other odds and ends.

(d) There were two reasons why Sebastian Ellis never went to parties his dislike of crowds and his enjoyment of work.

(e) The spy knew there was only one thing he could do now swallow his suicide pill so that he could tell nothing to his captors.

(f) What Jerry really liked about college was this the chance to be responsible for himself.

(g) The pools-winner's shopping-list was simple but expensive a large house, a smart car and a complete wardrobe of new clothes.

(h) These were his last words "I leave everything to you."

(i) Tom's favourite meal was breakfast and his favourite breakfast was always the same grapefruit, boiled egg, toast and coffee.

(j) The prisoners-of-war felt they had one main duty to escape.

Brackets

Brackets are always used in pairs and enclose information which is not part of the main meaning.

eg *This evening's canal cruise (tickets 50p) departs at 7.30 pm.*

There are many occasions when you could use either brackets or a pair of commas, eg:

The next aeroplane (a Boeing 707) landed on the far runway.

or *The next aeroplane, a Boeing 707, landed on the far runway.*

In cases like these, whether you use brackets or commas is up to you; on the whole, though, brackets are used when you want to keep the enclosed information rather more hidden away.

Brackets, however, differ from a pair of commas in that the information enclosed does not always fit naturally into the flow of the main sentence. In these cases you cannot use commas and only brackets are suitable, eg:

Further details (send stamped addressed envelope) are available from the Principal, Kirton Technical College, Kirton.

Exercise 114: Each of the sentences below contains information which is not part of the main meaning and which could be surrounded by brackets. (In several of the sentences you could equally well use commas, but in this exercise you are to use brackets only.) Write out each sentence, adding a pair of brackets in the correct place. Do not add any other punctuation.

Example: *Carbon tetrachloride CCl₄ is commonly used for dry-cleaning clothes.*

becomes *Carbon tetrachloride (CCl₄) is commonly used for dry-cleaning clothes.*

(a) The VC Victoria Cross was instituted in 1856 and is awarded for conspicuous bravery.

(b) The writer argues strongly chapter 3 that larger organisations are usually less efficient than smaller ones.

(c) For almost twenty years Sir Leonard Hutton held the record 364 for the highest score ever made in a Test Match.

(d) Her birthday 1st January always made it easy to calculate her age.

(e) Tickets £1.50 and £1 may be bought at the door.

(f) Please telephone the Fixtures Secretary Langdon 2784 if you need to find out whether a match has been cancelled.

(g) The moa illustration on page 72 was the largest of the flightless birds found in New Zealand.

(h) The exclamation mark ! should be used sparingly.

(i) The City Library 15 High Street has an excellent reference section.

(j) The kilogram 2.2 lbs is at last beginning to be accepted by British housewives.

Here are two more rules about using brackets:

A. When there are brackets in the same place as a punctuation mark belonging to the main sentence, that punctuation mark always comes after the second bracket, eg *The world's highest mountains are Everest (29 028 ft), K2 (28 250 ft) and Kanchenjunga (28 146 ft).* In this sentence both the comma and the full stop come after the brackets.

B. Unless a pair of brackets contains a complete sentence (or more than one sentence) which stands by itself and is not part of another sentence, you do not need to begin the words inside the brackets with a capital letter or end them with a full stop (though a question mark or exclamation mark is often used). Here are some examples:

The cold tap (I really must mend it) kept me awake by dripping loudly all through the night.

Quite by chance I met Hugh Ramsbotham (do you remember him?) on Tuesday.

Bill went to sleep (how typical!) straight after the meal.

By lunch-time the number of callers had quite exhausted Mary. (She had not slept well the previous night, anyway.) In the afternoon she decided to escape by going shopping.

In the last example the sentence in brackets stands on its own and not as part of another sentence. It is therefore punctuated as a complete sentence in itself.

Exercise 115: Punctuate the following sentences. To each sentence you will need to add: one pair of brackets, a final full stop and whatever punctuation may be necessary inside the brackets.

(a) The highest shade temperature recorded in Britain was 38°C 100.5°F in Kent in 1868
(b) The two comics, Thunder and Lightning Lightning is the thin one, made the audience laugh uproariously
(c) The cuckoo has arrived have you heard one yet so it must be spring
(d) To cross the bridge over the Avon motorists are required to pay a toll 5p
(e) Adrian didn't recognise Mrs Webster she had dyed her hair blonde until she told him who she was
(f) Mrs Tasker could not attend her daughter's wedding what a dreadful shame because she was in hospital
(g) The first successful gramophone was constructed by Thomas Alva Edison 1847-1931
(h) I wasn't sorry when Simon silly fool fell in the river
(i) The population of Albania is 2 616 000 1977 estimate
(j) For next week's party I need a pair of black boots, a bow tie can you lend me yours, some pin-striped trousers and a bowler hat

Dash

The dash has certain definite uses and should not be used instead of a full stop, semi-colon or comma.

There are four uses of the dash.

A.   The most common use is very similar to brackets: to enclose information which is not part of the main meaning of the sentence. For this purpose the dash, like brackets, is always used in pairs. The difference is that the dash gives a slight sense of abruptness and does not hide the information quite so thoroughly. Look at these two sentences:

For many years the Empire State Building (1472 feet) was the highest building in the world.
For many years the Empire State Building – it is 1472 feet high – was the highest building in the world.

You will find that dashes enclose complete sentences (as in the second example above) more frequently than brackets, but, as with brackets, these do not begin with a capital letter or end with a full stop. However, you must use question marks or exclamation marks if they are required, eg:

Charles looked out of the window – would it never stop raining? – and turned back to his books.

Exercise 116: Write out each of the following sentences, adding a pair of dashes and any other punctuation that is necessary between the dashes. (In many of the sentences you could equally well use brackets, but in this exercise you are to use only dashes.)

Example:

The speaker everybody could see it plainly was shaking with nerves.
becomes *The speaker — everybody could see it plainly — was shaking with nerves.*

(a) She looked down at the broken cup why was she so careless and went to get a cloth.

(b) The exhausted racing pigeon he thought it must be one of Mr Weston's sat motionless on the grass.

(c) Jack looked quickly over his shoulder had the policeman seen him and concentrated on walking calmly down the road.

(d) Alfie Sykes what a clumsy oaf had trodden on the sandwiches again.

(e) The men went back to work they had finally accepted the management's pay offer and the factory resumed full production.

(f) Terry looked carefully at the girl by the window had he seen her before and decided to go across and talk to her.

(g) Simon looked at his watch how late Jane always was and pulled his coat more tightly about him.

(h) The family emerged wearily from the shelter the all-clear had sounded and went slowly back into the house.

(i) During the night what a violent storm I hardly slept.

(j) That dress I'm sorry to be rude just does not suit you.

B.   The single dash is used, usually near the end of a sentence, to mark off a word or group of words which summarises or explains what the writer has been saying. A colon could often be used instead, but a comma would be either confusing or not strong enough.

Example:
   He went to discos for only one reason − to meet girls.

C.   In speech a single dash is used to show that the speaker has changed his mind about what he is going to say. There may be a series of dashes to show that he has changed his mind several times.

Example:
   "I'll take this one − no, that one − no, that one over there," said the customer.

D.   An interrupted and unfinished sentence usually ends with a dash (or a series of dots: ....), eg:

   Jason edged his way carefully across the pond. "You stay here," he explained, "while I − "
   "Look out!" shouted Terry. "The ice is cracking!"

Exercise 117:   Write out each of the following sentences, adding dashes where necessary. Do not add any other punctuation.

(a) Eleanor has one good quality above all she's always cheerful.
(b) "Let's put that poster behind the door no, over the table no, this is the best place."
(c) The mysterious meat-thief, caught in the act, stood there quite unashamed the next-door dog.
(d) She lay on her back at the top of the cliff and listened to the sound that always reminded her of her childhood the calling of the gulls.
(e) "The goal-keeper's saved it no, he's dropped it it's a goal!"
(f) He was sorry but the price of the ring was just too high over fifty pounds.
(g) "I'll tell you why we've got so few customers today there's a bus strike."
(h) "I'd like a pizza, please no, I'll change that to a steak no, I think I'll have spaghetti instead, thank you."
(i) "Let's cross the road now no, wait right, let's go."
(j) To be successful there's something you need more than brains hard work.

Hyphen

The hyphen is a shorter line than the dash; it joins together two parts of a word.

HYPHEN USED TO JOIN TOGETHER A WORD for which there is not enough space at the end of a line

If you need to write a word in two parts, with the second part at the beginning of a new line, you must link the parts with a hyphen — but you must be careful where you place it. The hyphen may be placed only between syllables (see EXPLANATION OF TERMS, page 136), eg *pavement, cross-ing*. Words of one syllable, therefore, eg: *road, car,* cannot be split.

The hyphen is placed between syllables to link two parts of a word for which there is not enough space at the end of a line.

You should always place the hyphen at the end of the first line (to show the reader that the word is incomplete) and not at the beginning of the next line.

Exercise 118: Below are twenty words, each containing a hyphen. Ten of the words are wrongly split. Write out all twenty words with the hyphen in the correct place. If the word is only one syllable (and therefore cannot be split), write it out with no hyphen.

Examples:
sunshi-ne becomes *sun-shine*; *li-ght* becomes *light*; *lan-tern* is written out exactly as it is because it is correct.

(a) cro-cus	(f) cup-board	(k) win-dow	(p) mo-nthly
(b) ro-se	(g) wardrob-e	(l) mach-ine	(q) rul-er
(c) pen-cil	(h) car-pet	(m) do-or	(r) kicke-d
(d) pe-n	(i) cu-rtain	(n) week-ly	(s) splash-ing
(e) paper-s	(j) r-ug	(o) fort-night	(t) divi-ng

HYPHEN USED TO MAKE ONE WORD OUT OF TWO

Quite often we need to write two words together as if they were one word. These are called compound words and the two (or more) parts of a compound word are joined by a hyphen. Here are two examples:

The sun streamed in through the half-open window.
Sharon earned several pounds each week as a baby-sitter.

In the first sentence we are not talking about a *half window* or an *open window*, but a *half-open window.* The hyphen is necessary to show this. In the second sentence *baby-sitter* is one of those common compound words like *pen-knife* and *table-cloth.*

Compound words are joined together by a hyphen.

Exercise 119: Each of the following sentences contains a compound word with the hyphen (or hyphens) left out. Write out each sentence, adding the hyphens in the correct place.

Example:
The drink was ice cold and very welcome. becomes *The drink was ice-cold and very welcome.*

(a) Wearily he bent down to tie his shoe laces.
(b) A red hot coal tumbled from the fire and lay smouldering on the carpet.
(c) The villain of the film was a baby faced gangster called Sylvester.
(d) The ancient stones reared towards the sky in an impressive semi circle.
(e) The moist atmosphere condensed on the window panes and ran down in untidy streams.
(f) Anna was always bright eyed and fresh faced. (*There are two compound words in this sentence.*)
(g) Forget me nots were Susie's favourite flowers.
(h) As usual, Mr Bellinger set off for home with a bulging brief case.
(i) The Kavanaghs lived in the pleasant Wiltshire town of Bradford on Avon.
(j) ''You're a two faced, double crossing horn swoggler!'' cried Hank angrily.
(*There are three compound words in this sentence.*)

COMMON ERRORS

This part of the book deals with the errors most commonly found in written English. Each error is explained clearly, with a minimum of technical terms, and there are examples and follow-up exercises on all the points covered.

How do we decide what is an error? What do we mean by the word 'correct'? In the end, the answer to these questions lies in the way people write and speak English. Usage determines the rules but there is often a difference between what some people regard as correct and the natural way in which English is used. For example, the sentence:

Who were you speaking to?

would be regarded as incorrect by some people for two reasons: the sentence ends with a preposition, and the first word should be *whom*, since it comes after a preposition, *to*. The sentence would then become

To whom were you speaking?

Although grammatically correct, this sentence sounds to many people — including the writers of this book — uneasy and unnatural. If the two rules mentioned above are strictly followed, even more unnatural sentences are produced, eg *Out with whom did you go last night?*

This does not mean that we can or should disregard rules whenever we feel like it. Certain rules must be followed and you will find only these mentioned in this part of the book. These rules lead to written English which is both correct and natural.

Misplaced words

If you are not careful, you may put words in the wrong position in a sentence. In the following example,

She wanted to have her hair done badly.

the word *badly* is misplaced. It should go with the word *wanted* and the sentence should be written:

She badly wanted to have her hair done.

The rule, therefore, is:

All words must be placed with the part of the sentence they refer to.

This rule is particularly important when you are dealing with phrases that have verbs ending in *-ing*. For example, in this sentence,

She found her purse walking down the street.

it is not the *purse* that is doing the *walking,* but *she.* Therefore the sentence must be rearranged thus:

Walking down the street, she found her purse.

Exercise 120:   To the following sentence:

I wanted to see Mr Spencer about my son.

the word *only* has been added and appears in different positions. What is the difference in meaning in each case?

(a)   Only I wanted to see Mr Spencer about my son.
(b)   I only wanted to see Mr Spencer about my son.
(c)   I wanted to see only Mr Spencer about my son.
(d)   I wanted to see Mr Spencer only about my son.
(e)   I wanted to see Mr Spencer about my only son.

Exercise 121:   Each of the following sentences has a misplaced word or phrase. Rewrite each sentence so that the words are in the right place. In some cases you will have to add some words.

(a)   He wanted to play the guitar badly.
(b)   Chambermaid required. Must be respectable until September.
(c)   My uncle shot the elephant in his pyjamas.
(d)   Piano for sale by lady with carved legs.
(e)   Hanging round her neck, he saw the silver necklace.
(f)   She paid the milkman still wearing a dressing gown.
(g)   Room to let. Suitable for young person 20 foot by 15 foot.
(h)   Headache? Let us examine your eyes and remove same.
(i)   Flying in the air, houses look funny.
(j)   On the expedition I hunted and shot myself.
(k)   Sports car wanted by young man with MOT.

One word or two?

It is sometimes difficult to know whether certain words should be joined up or written separately. Here are some guidelines.

A. **One word**
The following are always written as a single word:

   (i)   a number of words beginning *to-*
        Examples: *today*   *together*
                        tonight   *tomorrow*
  (ii) words ending in *-self* or *-selves*
        Examples: *myself*   *ourselves*
                        yourself   *yourselves*
                        himself, herself *themselves*
                        itself
 (iii) certain other words: *unless, until, cannot, without, instead*

B. **Two words**
Notice that the following are always written as separate words:

                    thank you   *a lot of*
                    on to   *in front*
                    all right   *in fact*

C. **Either one word or two**
Some words may be written as one or two words depending on the sense.
For example:

    all ready means *everything or everyone is ready*
    already means *before now* or *previously*

Other examples of words which are written as one or two depending on the meaning are:

   all ways/always   *all together/altogether*
   may be/maybe   *in to/into*
   no body/nobody   *some times/sometimes*
   any one/anyone   *every one/everyone*

Exercise 122: Decide which of the alternatives in each sentence is correct.

(a) I'm already/all ready late for the party.
(b) They were already/all ready.
(c) She's already/all ready seen the doctor.
(d) I've always/all ways loved her.
(e) He considered always/all ways of escaping.
(f) He always/all ways wanted to write something for his son.
(g) You could always/all ways try slimming.
(h) The papers are altogether/all together in the file.
(i) She came back altogether/all together different.
(j) I don't altogether/all together agree with you.
(k) Shall I put them altogether/all together?
(l) That maybe/may be the answer.
(m) Maybe/may be she'll ring tomorrow.
(n) The judge went into/in to the evidence carefully.
(o) He went into/in to see what had happened.
(p) After a period uranium turns into/in to lead.
(q) There was nobody/no body in the coffin.
(r) She was upset because nobody/no body came to her party.
(s) Sometimes/some times you are not truthful.
(t) There are sometimes/some times when it is not tactful to be truthful.

Exercise 123: Write out correctly any words which are wrongly spelled in the sentences below.

(a) She did it all by her self.
(b) Leave that until next week.
(c) I can not understand why you said that.
(d) You'll suffer for this tomorrow.
(e) Thankyou very much for the invitation.
(f) He always gets into alot of trouble.
(g) Unless you do more training, you'll never win.
(h) They were not good at working to gether.
(i) We'll finish it ourselves.
(j) I couldnot possibly agree to that.
(k) What are you doing to night?
(l) Do you think it will be alright?
(m) The cat jumped onto the table.
(n) I cannot go on without her.

Past tenses

There are two main methods of describing events that have happened in the past.

One method is to put the verb into the simple past tense (see EXPLANATION OF TERMS, page 136). You can often do this by adding -ed to the basic verb, eg *I kick the ball* becomes *I kicked the ball.* But there are many verbs which do not follow this pattern.

Examples:
see	-	*Yesterday I saw him*
drive	-	*He drove home last night*
take	-	*We took some photos last week*

The other method is to put *have, has* or *had* in front of the past participle of the verb. Again, although *I kick the ball* becomes *I have kicked the ball,* many verbs have irregular past participles.

Examples:
see	-	*I have seen him often*
drive	-	*He has driven many miles*
take	-	*We had taken the wrong turning*

Here is a list of some common verbs which sometimes cause difficulties in the past tense.

Verb	Simple past	Past with *have/had/has*
begin	*began*	*begun*
come	*came*	*come*
do	*did*	*done*
drink	*drank*	*drunk*
drive	*drove*	*driven*
go	*went*	*gone*
ring	*rang*	*rung*
run	*ran*	*run*
see	*saw*	*seen*
show	*showed*	*shown*
sing	*sang*	*sung*
speak	*spoke*	*spoken*
swim	*swam*	*swum*
take	*took*	*taken*
tear	*tore*	*torn*

Exercise 124:   Put the verb in brackets into the past.

(a) I (take) twenty minutes to get here.
(b) How many pictures have you (take)?
(c) She's (take) a long time.
(d) What (take) you so long?
(e) I have (ring) you twice today.
(f) Who (ring) the doorbell?
(g) They've (ring) off.
(h) She (ring) for the porter.
(i) Have you (see) him?
(j) He (drive) me home.
(k) She'd (swim) the Channel before.
(l) That's (tear) it.

Exercise 125:   Write out correctly any of the following sentences which are wrong.

(a) You shouldn't have spoke to him like that.
(b) She had often sung with that group.
(c) You might have showed more sympathy.
(d) When she run out of the room, she tore her dress.
(e) It had just began to snow.
(f) They went to Spain and drunk too much.
(g) Last week our team was beat 2-0.

Some tricky verbs

These groups of verbs sometimes cause difficulties.

A. *Lie/lay*
   The verb *to lie* has two meanings:
   (i) *to tell a lie, something untrue*
   (ii) *to lie down or recline*

Lie never takes an object; you can never *lie* something.
The verb *to lay* means *to put down*. It can take an object.

Example:
   They laid the carpet last week.

B. *Rise/raise*
   To rise means *to go up, to increase,* etc. It does not take an object.
   To raise means *to lift up* or cause to go up. You always *raise*
   something.

C. *Hang*
   This verb has two uses:
   (i) *to be supported from above* (like a lamp, picture)
   (ii) *to put to death (in a certain way)*

You must be particularly careful when using any of the above verbs in
the past tense. The past tense varies according to the meaning.

Verb	Simple past	Past with *have/had/has*
lie (to recline)	*lay*	*lain*
lie (to tell a lie)	*lied*	*lied*
lay (to put down)	*laid*	*laid*
rise (to go up)	*rose*	*risen*
raise (to lift up)	*raised*	*raised*
hang (to be supported from above)	*hung*	*hung*
hang (to put to death)	*hanged*	*hanged*

Exercise 126:   Put *lie* or *lay* in the following blanks.

(a)   ..... down for a while.
(b)   ..... down your weapons.
(c)   Will you please ..... the table?
(d)   Let sleeping dogs ..... .
(e)   I can't ..... my hands on it.
(f)   Don't ..... to me.

Exercise 127:   Put *rise* or *raise* in the following blanks.

(a)   Prices ..... every day.
(b)   The firm had to ..... its prices.
(c)   The bread won't ..... .
(d)   Can we ..... a loan?
(e)   Don't ..... your voice.
(f)   When does the moon .....?

Exercise 128:   Write out correctly any of the following sentences that are wrong.

(a)   She was lain low by flu.
(b)   The river has already raised two feet.
(c)   The firm laid off fifty workers.
(d)   The prisoner was hanged for murder.
(e)   The temperature has rose 20 degrees.
(f)   She hanged the washing in the garden.
(g)   He lied to me about the money.
(h)   Who laid the table yesterday?
(i)   We rose an objection to the plan.
(j)   They lay quite still until the soldiers passed.

Prepositions

You must always try to avoid using any of the following:

A.   **The wrong preposition** (see EXPLANATION OF TERMS, page 136)
Here are the correct forms of some common mistakes:

different **from**	and not	*different* **than**
opposite or *opposite* **to**	and not	*opposite* **from**
fed up **with**	and not	*fed up* **of**
depend **on**	and not	*depend* **of**

And remember—do **not** write *of* when it should be *have,* as in the
sentence:
You should **have** *come.*

B.   **Unnecessary prepositions**
In each of the following examples the preposition(s) in bold type are
not needed and should be left out.
It fell off **of** *the table.*
Where is he going **to***?*
Is the match over **with***?*
It's not clear **as to** *what happened.*
He lives near **to** *the college.*
Where is the party **at***?*

Note: *To comprise* means *to consist of.* You should never write
comprise of.
Either   *This course* **comprises** *five main parts.*
or   *This course* **consists of** *five main parts.*

114

Exercise 129: In the sentences below put in the correct preposition where one is necessary.

(a) The committee consisted ..... ten members.
(b) My handwriting is different ..... yours.
(c) They live in the bungalow opposite ..... yours.
(d) It all depends ..... his exam results.
(e) The situation today is different ..... what it used to be.
(f) I am fed up ..... his behaviour.
(g) My sister's hair is a different colour ..... mine.
(h) The force comprised ..... two battalions.

Exercise 130: All the following sentences have unnecessary prepositions. Which are they?

(a) Where are you going to tomorrow?
(b) I'll meet you outside of the cinema.
(c) The jockey fell off of the horse.
(d) I'd like to live near to the sea.
(e) He asked us as to what we had seen.
(f) Where has she been at all day?
(g) Eigg is an island off of the Scottish coast.
(h) Is the storm over with yet?
(i) I got off of the train at Wolverhampton.
(j) Have you any idea as to what happened?

Agreement: subject and object

In this sentence:

Later that evening he kissed her.

he is called the **subject** because the man is doing the action – the kissing. This makes the woman the **object** of the sentence and therefore we use the form *her*. If the roles are changed and the woman does the action, then we have to write *she kissed him.*

Here is a list of the forms you must use, depending on whether these words are the subject or object of the sentence:

Subject	Object
I	*me*
he	*him*
she	*her*
we	*us*
they	*them*
who	*whom*

Note: *you* and *it* do not change.

You must always use the object-form after a preposition.

Examples:

by **us** (not *we*)

between you and **me** (not *I*)

except you and **him** (not *he*)

Note: It is more polite to write

you and I	rather than	*I and you*
she and I	rather than	*I and she*

Put the *I* second.

Exercise 131: Say whether *Barry* is the subject or object in each of these sentences and then substitute *he* or *him* for *Barry*.

(a) Barry and I paid the bill.
(b) The bill was paid by Barry.
(c) Susan and Barry are going together.
(d) Barry spilled the soup.
(e) Nobody was late except Barry.

Exercise 132: Put *I* or *me* into each of these blanks.

(a) Did you hear about Jill and ....?
(b) She met .... at the station.
(c) Then Jill and ..... went to a party.
(d) She and .... had an argument.
(e) Jill said .... was to blame.
(f) As for .... , ... thought it was her fault.
(g) It never occurred to .... that .... was wrong.
(h) She said she never wanted to see the likes of .... again.
(i) .... don't know what's going to happen to Jill and .... .

Exercise 133: Write out correctly any of these sentences which are wrong.

(a) She and I will do the washing-up.
(b) I am proud of you and he.
(c) Everyone knows the news except me.
(d) I'm going to the concert with Dan and she.
(e) I and you can take care of that.
(f) It's a matter between us and them.
(g) They gave my friend and I some good advice.
(h) Me and Tom fixed the car.
(i) There are no secrets between my sister and me.
(j) That's the person with who I had the argument.
(k) My girl-friend and I are getting engaged.
(l) They invited Jim and I to dinner.

Agreement: singular and plural

Some words are always singular, some always plural and some may be either.

A. Singular
The following words are always singular and take a singular verb:

anyone/anybody	*someone/somebody*
everyone/everybody	*one*
no one/nobody	*each*

Example:
Each of his men **has** *finished.* (not *have*)

B. Plural
These words are always plural and take a plural verb:
   many   both   few   several   others

Example:
A few of them **have** *finished.* (not *has*)

C. Either singular or plural
The following words may be either singular or plural. There are no definite rules to tell you which form to use, but normally the sense and sound will guide you.
   all   any   some   none

Example:
None of us **has** *finished.* or *None of us* **have** *finished.*

Note: Many nouns describing a group or collection of people fall into this category. All these nouns, for example, can be either singular or plural, depending on the sense in which they are being used.

government	*family*
committee	*staff*
department	*audience*
office	*crowd*

Be careful not to use any of these nouns as both singular and plural in the same sentence.

Exercise 134: Complete this sentence using each of the words below and decide whether you should put *is* (singular) or *are* (plural) in each case.

.... of them is/are prepared to go.

(a) both
(b) one
(c) each
(d) several

(e) many
(f) every one
(g) a few
(h) none

Exercise 135: Write out correctly each of the sentences below which is incorrect.

(a) Each of these examples include a number of mistakes.
(b) Both of the men came with his tools.
(c) All of them were waiting for their tickets.
(d) If anyone is looking for their books, I've got them.
(e) Each one is expected to do their best.
(f) Someone has left his jacket.
(g) Several of them are going abroad for their holidays.
(h) Both she and her sister has passed their test.
(i) Everyone could make themselves heard.

Exercise 136: Remembering that the subject of a sentence must always agree with its verb, state which of these sentences have faulty singular/plural agreement and write them out correctly.

(a) One single and one double room was available.
(b) The demand for higher wages has led to an increase in prices.
(c) The timetable for flights to Spain appear in our latest brochure.
(d) Most purchases in a supermarket is made on impulse.
(e) The subjects for the new course are given in the College prospectus.
(f) Standards of living have fallen in many countries.
(g) The temptation for young people to drink and smoke is very great.
(h) The family are all well and send its best wishes.

Ambiguity

In this sentence,

Jane told Tracy that she had passed.

who passed? Was it Jane or Tracy? It is impossible to tell from the sentence as it stands. This is called ambiguity. It happens particularly when words like *he/him, she/her, it* and *they/them* come after two people are mentioned at the beginning of a sentence.

There are a number of ways of getting rid of the ambiguity. If Jane was the person who passed, we could write

Jane passed and told Tracy.
or *When Jane had passed, she told Tracy.*
or *Jane told Tracy, "I've passed."*
Another way, which is clear but awkward, is:

Jane told Tracy that she (Jane) had passed.

Exercise 137: In each of the following sentences get rid of the ambiguity in your own way by making clear that the name in brackets is the name referred to:

Example:

Bill asked his brother where he had put the money. (His brother)
could become *Bill asked where his brother had put the money.*

(a) John told Martin he was useless. (Martin)
(b) Mary asked June if it was her fault. (June)
(c) Craig told his friend that it was his turn to pay. (His friend)
(d) Tom's father is a millionaire and this makes him very pleased with himself. (Tom)
(e) Sue told her sister that she could never love Humphrey. (Sue)
(f) Although the match between the staff and students was close, they deserved to win. (The staff)
(g) Gail had an argument with Sally before she left. (Gail)
(h) Ray went to see Jim and rode his Yamaha. (Ray)
(i) Pat decided to tell her cousin that she was making a big mistake. (Her cousin)
(j) Because I learned it as a child, I can now speak French and Spanish fluently. (French)

HANDWRITING

First impressions are very important. A reader's first impression of something written by you will be given by the neatness and pleasantness of your handwriting and layout.

A strong and continuing part of this first impression will be the ease with which your reader finds he can read your handwriting. However intelligent your ideas, a reader will not be inclined to accept them if reading is a struggle and his progress through what you have written is jerky.

It is likely that markers of examination papers, for example, however fair they are consciously, are unconsciously influenced by the ease with which they can read the answers you have written. This is probably particularly true in subjects like English. This unconscious (and sometimes conscious) reaction to handwriting will be true in varying degrees of everything which you write in your own hand — whether it is a letter of application or a love-letter.

The first and main requirement of handwriting, therefore, is that it must be **legible** (readable).

Closely linked with legibility is the second requirement: handwriting must be of **pleasant appearance.** Legible but ugly writing will not produce a favourable reaction from the reader.

Before we look at some of the factors which make handwriting legible and of pleasant appearance, it ought to be said that the style of your handwriting has almost certainly been formed by the time you have reached the final years of secondary school and probably long before that point. However, by making a conscious effort with everything you write over a period of two or three weeks and a continuing but slightly less conscious effort for a longer period after that, **you can, if necessary, modify your handwriting so that it is more legible and more pleasant to read.**

Since handwriting is of such vital importance, it is worth your while to make this effort if you need to. It will improve your ability to communicate effectively and it may have a considerable influence on your future.

It is not being suggested that you should change your whole style of handwriting — merely that you should, if necessary, alter it in such a way that it becomes more easily legible and more pleasant to read.

The main factors influencing the legibility and pleasant appearance of handwriting are **slope, shape, size** and **spacing.** Examine your handwriting in the light of what is written about these factors on the next three pages and decide how you can improve it.

(i) Slope

Letters may slope forwards or backwards or they may be upright. Two points are important:

Letters should not slope too much in any direction, eg:

these letters slope backwards too much

and the slope should not vary from letter to letter, eg:

these letters slope differently

Here is an example of good sloping:

these letters slope pleasantly

(ii) Shape

All letters should be written with **the correct shape.** The more the letters look alike, the more difficult it will be for your reader to understand what you have written. Handwriting like this:

is usually difficult to read

because there is not enough difference between the letters.

The correct shape of letters is particularly important **when they can easily be confused.** For example, when writing *e* and *i*, do not write like this:

letter

because it is not clear whether the word is *letter* or *litter*. (*i* should, of course, be dotted but this is sometimes not done.)

The correct shape is also important **when joining up letters.** For example, is the following word

bottle

meant to be *battle* or *bottle*? Because the second letter has not been clearly shaped when joined to the third letter, it is impossible to tell. Remember to write either:

battle or *bottle*

(iii) Size

Letters should be **the correct size.**

They should not be too big, eg:

these letters are too big

nor too small, eg:

these letters are too small

nor should they be all the same height. Letters should be either tall or short — and some go beneath the line. These differences should be made clear, eg:

't' - tall ; 's' - short ; 'g' - below line

   Make sure that your letters are uniform in size and that their overall size is both economical to write and easy to read. For example:

this is about the right size

(iv) Spacing

It does not matter whether you join together all the letters in a word or whether some are separate. You should always make sure, however,

that there are no large gaps between letters, eg:

don 't lea ve g aps be twe en l ett ers

123

and that there are not unequal spaces between words, eg:

don't leave   uneven   spaces between   words

Be careful also to leave **the same space between lines and paragraphs.**

Alterations

As a general rule you should, of course, try to avoid making mistakes when writing, particularly mistakes caused by spelling, missed-out words, etc. It is, however, inevitable that you will from time to time make mistakes and, when this happens, you will have to do one of the following:

A.   Re-write the page containing the mistake (or mistakes). This will have to be done with any important piece of writing, eg a letter of application for a job, an essay or project which is assessed as part of a course, etc.

B.   Cross out the wrong word (or words) with a single, horizontal line and write the correct word(s) just above or after the mistake. This type of correction is suitable for writing which will not be examined or which is not intended for public viewing, eg a personal letter to a friend, lecture notes, etc. When writing corrections, do not put crosses or surround the mistake with brackets.

Exercise 138:   Below are examples of different handwriting. You will find some of them easy to read and others very difficult (if not impossible). Bearing in mind the points mentioned on the previous pages, look at these examples and decide for yourself which handwriting is good and which is bad — and for what reasons.

a).

If you have any problem, please don't hesitate to contact us. We are always willing to help.

b). He found a farmer willing to rent him a field and employed small boys to run round the streets telling people of the great display.

c). For many children in countries spread throughout the world the first foreign language that they learn is English.

d). Rocks are composed of minerals or of fragments of older rocks which are also made up of older rocks.

e). The characters should also be written fairly small, as a large and sprawling style is a waste of paper.

LAYOUT

The neat and correct setting out of what you write is very important for the same reasons as good handwriting is important (see page 121).

A reader must be able to understand your meaning clearly and easily and he must find himself actively wanting to read and understand what you have written.

Under no circumstances must he be put off by finding — or suspecting that he will find — any difficulty in following what is in front of him.

Moreover, setting out correctly what you write is a vital exercise for you, the writer. It forces you to work out in your own mind the logical order and organisation of your ideas. When you have done this and arranged your layout accordingly, you will be telling the reader the structure of your ideas by the way they are set out.

For these reasons correct layout is essential. It is much easier to learn the few principles of correct layout than it is to reach the stage of making no mistakes in spelling and punctuation — yet a surprisingly large number of people continue to write letters, reports, essays, etc that put their readers off both by their first appearance and by their confused organisation.

Although it requires clear thought, correct layout is not difficult — and it is essential.

Writing in paragraphs

When you write something of any length, ie containing more than one main idea, it is helpful to the reader if you divide what you write into paragraphs.

The reader will see that you have organised your ideas into a logical structure and will feel more confident of understanding what you have written. He will also not be put off by the dense mass of writing that would face him if there were no paragraphs.

Paragraphs will vary in length depending on what is being written. Very complicated ideas may require long paragraphs, very simple ideas perhaps paragraphs of only one sentence.

How to show where a new paragraph begins

A.   For the printed word (typed or printed material)

Either miss a line or start in from the margin.

The rule used to be that every paragraph should begin in from the margin. It is becoming increasingly common and acceptable, however, especially in business letters, for paragraphs to begin at the margin like every other line. The fact that it is a new paragraph must, of course, be shown and this is done by leaving a line between each paragraph.

This is called a blocked layout and you can see an example of this in the letter on page 131.

B.   For handwriting

Start in from the margin.

This is the old rule and it is still correct for handwriting. Every line that you write must start immediately underneath the one above (a common fault which must be avoided is for margins to wander) **except** the first line of a new paragraph, which should start in (about 25 mm) from the margin. Each new paragraph should start exactly the same distance in from the margin and a line should not be left between paragraphs.

In this book, as in most books, we have shown new paragraphs by starting in from the margin (since it would be expensive to leave a blank line between every paragraph in a whole book). You can, of course, see examples on this and the opposite page.

Headings and sub-headings

There are no rules about how to write headings and sub-headings. However, as with all aspects of layout, **you must follow a consistent and logical pattern.**

You may have only one heading for what you write or, as is often the case with notes or reports, you may have several headings of differing degrees of importance. For example, if you were on page 16 of this book, the **part** you were on would be called Spelling (heading p. 7), the **section** would be Section 1: Sight and sound (heading p. 8) and the **unit** would be Same-sounding words (heading top of p. 16). To indicate their ranking they have been printed in different ways and you will find that there is a consistent pattern of headings and sub-headings throughout this book. The unit heading at the top of this page, for example, is printed in the same style as the unit heading just quoted.

It is slightly less easy to vary the writing of headings in handwriting or typewriting than it is in printing, but it is still possible. For example, your headings in a typed essay or survey might be as follows:

TRAFFIC CONGESTION IN THE TOWN CENTRE

THE PROBLEM

Cyclists

Cars

Heavy vehicles

Pedestrians

THE SOLUTION

etc ....

In this example capital and small letters, a heading in the centre and headings starting at the margin have been used to vary the style and show the different degrees of importance.

Note that with a blocked layout (ie all paragraphs starting at the margin – see A on previous page) it is usual for all headings as well as all paragraphs to be blocked. In other words, there will be no centred headings and they will all start at the margin like the paragraphs.

Numbering and lettering

Sometimes it is helpful to the reader to number or letter the parts of what you are writing, especially when there are many items. The numbering or lettering may be linked with your headings or there may be no headings.

Although there is no rule about how to number or letter, **you must follow a consistent and logical pattern.**

There are several possibilities:

1, 2, 3, 4 etc
i, ii, iii, iv etc
I, II, III, IV etc
A, B, C, D etc
a, b, c, d, etc

and other variations of these, with or without brackets, with or without underlining.

In this book you will see that we have **numbered** the exercises, and **lettered** the items in each exercise, often from (a) to (j). We have also made occasional use of (i), (ii) etc and of A, B, etc.

If you wished to number and letter the example of headings on the previous page, you might do it like this:

TRAFFIC CONGESTION IN THE TOWN CENTRE

1. THE PROBLEM

    (a) Cyclists

    (b) Cars

    (c) Heavy vehicles

    (d) Pedestrians

2. THE SOLUTION

    (a) etc ....

As you can see, it is up to you how (and if) you number or letter the parts of what you write. You must, however, follow a consistent and logical pattern — and do not be too complicated.

Exercise 139: Below are the headings, sub-headings, etc of a proposal put forward by the student council of a college for improvements to the college timetable. Do not change the order of the headings but set them out on the page in the clearest possible way, using capital letters, small letters and underlining to give the right degree of importance to each heading. Number and/or letter each heading as you think most suitable.

suggested improvements to the college timetable / the origins of the present timetable / disadvantages of the present timetable / long periods of free time / clashes of some subjects / Audio-typing and English / Audio-typing and French / Engineering Drawing and English / inflexibility / a possible new timetable / a suggested schedule for introducing a new timetable / immediate action / longer-term planning.

Writing letters

Letters are set out in either of two layouts: **blocked,** which is increasingly common with typed business letters, or **traditional,** which is still normal for handwritten letters.

A.   Blocked layout

There is no indenting of paragraphs, nor do addresses slope. The blocked layout is usually accompanied by what is called open punctuation, ie full stops are left out after abbreviations (see page 70) and commas are left out of addresses and dates and after the first and final greetings (see pages 83 and 84). Although there is no definite rule, we recommend **the blocked layout (and open punctuation) for typed letters**.

Below is an example of a short business letter set out in this way. Note the correct positioning of the address of the writer, the date, the address of the person to whom the letter is being sent and the first and final greeting.

A P Weston & Co Ltd
22 City Road
Brighton
Sussex

12 November 1981

Mr J Lambert
14 Hinton Road
Spilsborough
Sussex

Dear Mr Lambert

Thank you for your letter of application received this morning for the vacant post of storeman. I should be pleased if you could attend for interview at 10.30 am on Wednesday 18 November.

Yours sincerely

T Watkinson
Personnel Manager

Exercise 140: Set out the following business letter in a blocked layout with open punctuation as if it were typed. You will need to add some punctuation marks in the body of the letter; it would also be advisable to start a new paragraph for the final sentence.

29 Western Avenue Kilham Lancs 14 December 1981 The Manager Kilham Catering Ltd Trading Estate Kilham Lancs Dear Sir You undertook to supply refreshments for approximately 1500 spectators last Saturday 12 December There were in fact just under 1000 spectators but there was sufficient food and drink for only about 500 I should be grateful if you would telephone me at Kilham 5312 to discuss the matter Yours faithfully P Lenham Hon Sec Kilham Football Club

B. Traditional layout
Again, as with the blocked layout, there is no definite rule but we recommend **the traditional layout for handwritten letters.**

Below is an example of a handwritten letter set out in the traditional layout. Note the sloping address of the writer, the position of the date, the indented paragraphs and the position of the final greeting.

> Flat 5,
> 128, London Road,
> Burminster.
> 28th April 1981
>
> Dear Alison,
> I am sorry I was out when you called yesterday.
> Thank you for leaving a note.
> Would you and Steve like to come round for a meal on Saturday evening? We would very much like to see you both.
> Love,
> Jenny

Exercise 141: Set out the letter below in a traditional layout, adding all the necessary punctuation.

Stanton College Stanton Tuesday 3rd March Dear Mr Brotherton I am writing on behalf of the College Social Committee to apologise for the disturbance caused by the disco last Wednesday Until you telephoned the Principal we had no idea that we had made so much noise and we apologise most sincerely It will not happen again I hope we shall see you at next week's meeting of the Drama Club as usual Yours sincerely Peter Mullis Hon Sec Stanton College Social Committee.

Writing direct speech

The layout of direct speech has already been explained in the unit on speech marks (see page 89). The rule is:

New speaker, new line.

This means that every time there is a change of speakers you must begin on a new line and in from the margin. You are, in fact, starting a new paragraph.

There is an example of this on page 89 as well as an exercise; further practice is given in the exercise which follows.

Exercise 142:   Write out the following conversation, adding no punctuation but starting each new speaker on a new line and in from the margin.

"Would you like an ice-cream?" John asked as the lights went up for the interval. "No thanks," said Pat. "Would you?" "No, I don't want one either. In fact, I'd like to go," said John. "Why?" asked Pat. "Aren't you enjoying this film?" "I'm afraid not," said John. "I think it's badly acted and unnecessarily violent. I'm not enjoying it at all." There was a pause before Pat said, "Well, I think I agree with you." She reached under the seat for her bag and got to her feet. "Let's go then, John. It's a bit of a waste of money but there's no point sitting here not enjoying ourselves." John smiled at her. "Thank you," he said.

Quotations

You will sometimes need to use quotations, especially when you are writing about a book, play, film, etc. This is how quotations should be set out.

PROSE

Almost all quotations except very long ones
Continue writing along the same line with the quotation forming a normal part of the sentence, except that it will be enclosed in speech marks, eg:

>Churchill could offer the country only "blood, toil, tears and sweat".

Very long quotations
The quotation is started on a new line and, to show clearly that it is a quotation, it is best to start all the lines of the passage quoted slightly in from the left-hand margin. Because of this way of setting out the words, they are obviously a quotation — so do not use speech marks. When the quotation is completed, you begin again on a new line at the left-hand side of the page, eg:

>On 20th August 1940 Winston Churchill addressed the House of Commons in these words:
>>The gratitude of every home in our island, in our Empire, and indeed throughout the world, except in the abodes of the guilty, goes out to the British airmen who, undaunted by odds, unwearied in their constant challenge and mortal danger, are turning the tide of the world war by their prowess and by their devotion. Never in the field of human conflict was so much owed by so many to so few.
>The battle in the air of which Churchill was speaking became known as the Battle of Britain and the British airmen who fought in it were called the Few.

POETRY

Less than one line of verse
As with shorter prose quotations, continue writing along the same line

with the quotation forming a normal part of the sentence, except that it will be enclosed in speech marks, eg:

D H Lawrence despised his "accursed human education" which made him throw a log at the snake.

One line of verse or more

The quotation is started on a new line and written as lines of verse, with any half-lines in the correct place. Begin each line of verse slightly in from the left-hand margin. Because of the way they are set out, the words are obviously a quotation — so do not use speech marks. When the quotation is completed, you begin again on a new line at the left-hand side of the page, eg:

To D H Lawrence the snake symbolised a side of life which modern man has lost, an elemental and passionate side which the world needs to rediscover:

> *For he seemed to me again like a king,*
> *Like a king in exile, uncrowned in the underworld,*
> *Now due to be crowned again.*

The poem ends with Lawrence bitterly regretting his petty rejection of the snake and feeling that he must atone for his action.

Note: It is possible to have direct speech within a quotation (or a quotation within direct speech). In this case the second pair of speech marks should be turned into a pair of single inverted commas, eg:

On 18th June 1940 Churchill said: "Let us therefore brace ourselves to our duties and so bear ourselves that, if the British Empire and its Commonwealth last for a thousand years, men will still say, 'This was their finest hour.' "

EXPLANATION OF TERMS

Here is a brief explanation of all the special terms used in this book.

Adjective: a word describing a noun (eg *an* **intelligent** *child* or *a* **busy** *town*)

Adverb: a word which tells more about a verb (eg *he arrived* **safely** or *start* **immediately)**

Consonant: any letter of the alphabet which is not a vowel (eg *b, c, m, z*)

Noun: the name of a thing (eg *boat, moon*), place (eg *Manchester, Mount Everest*), person (eg *Sally, Mr Edwards*) or quality (eg *patience, speed*)

Prefix: an addition at the beginning of a word (eg **dis***like*, **dis***appear*, **mis***use*, **mis***take*)

Preposition: a small word usually before a noun (eg **by** *car* or **to** *London*)

Suffix: an addition at the end of a word (eg *hope***ful***, cheer***ful***, break***able***, agree***able***)

Syllable: a word or part of a word made by a single effort of the voice; a syllable consists of one vowel sound (eg *school* has one vowel sound and is one syllable; *tel-e-phone* has three syllables; *mis-un-·der-stand-ing* has five syllables)

Tense: the past, present or future form of a verb (eg *I go* = present tense; *I have gone* or *I went* = past tense; *I shall go* = future tense)

Verb: a word which tells what somebody or something does (eg *she* **speaks** or *the sun* **rises**)

Vowel: the letters *a, e, i, o, u;* every word must have at least one vowel in it. The letter *y* is sometimes used as a vowel and sometimes as a consonant.

ANSWERS

This final part of the book contains answers to all the exercises. It is intended for use especially by those following a self-study course.

Spelling

Checking Exercise IA: Going from the top downwards, Diagram B has: 1. Straight line in circle at top of meter; 2. one arrow missing from FLAG; 3. 4 instead of 45 on time scale; 4. black portion on CLOCK-STARTER; 5. RACHET instead of RATCHET; 6. no arrow at end of RATCHET SLIDE; 7. no teeth on INDICATOR; 8. RESET LEVERS instead of RESET LEVER; 9. the word PAWL missing; 10. bottom section of INDICATOR missing; 11. top circle of TIME-INTERVAL ECCENTRIC missing; 12. the word CRANK missing after RESET BELL.

Exercise 1:   (a) to; to; too;   (b) to; to   (c) to   (d) to   (e) to; too

Exercise 2:   (a) two-tone   (b) two-ply   (c) two-stroke   (d) two-piece (e) two-faced

Exercise 3:   (a) too   (b) too   (c) two; to   (d) two   (e) Too   (f) too (g) two; two; to   (h) To; to   (i) Too; to   (j) two; to; two; too

Exercise 4:   (a) your; you're   (b) your; you're   (c) You're; your   (d) You're; your   (e) Your; you're   (f) You're; your

Exercise 5:   (a) your   (b) Yours   (c) You're; your   (d) yours   (e) your; you're   (f) yours

Exercise 6:   (a) Whose   (b) Who's   (c) Who's   (d) whose (e) whose   (f) who's

Exercise 7
(a)   your cold feet; you're cold
(b)   your kind offer; you're very kind
(c)   your own flat; you're flat (eg singing)
(d)   your left hand; you're left-handed
(e)   your back; you're back at last

Exercise 8:   (a) there; they're; their   (b) there; their; they're   (c) their; there; they're   (d) there; their; they're.   (e) there; their; they're

Exercise 9: (a) they're (b) their (c) there (d) they're (e) there
(f) their (g) there (h) there, there

Exercise 10: (a) theirs (b) There's (c) Theirs (d) There's (e) theirs
(f) there's

Exercise 11: (a) they're (b) There's; there (c) there (d) their (e) there's;
there's (f) They're; there; their

Exercise 12: (a)(i) current; (ii) currant (b) (i) naval; (ii) navel (c) (i) berth;
(ii) birth (d) (i) prey; (ii) pray (e) (i) course; (ii) coarse (f)(i) dual; (ii) duel

Exercise 13: (a) cheque (b) aisle (c) site (d) fair (e) brake (f) Where
(g) right (h) peace (i) sale (j) mail (k) lead (l) cell (m) ore (n) serial
(o) weather (p) board (q) idle (r) magnate (s) bye

Exercise 14: (a) maid (b) whole (c) knew (d) flour (e) bear (f) foul
(g) waist (h) berry (i) plane (j) bold

Checking Exercise IB
(i) (a) same (b) same (c) same (d) different (e) same (f) different
(g) different (h) same (i) different (j) same (k) same (l) different
(m) different (n) different (o) same (p) same (q) different (r) same
(ii) (b), (c), (e), (g), (h), (j), (l), (n), (q)
(iii) (a) & (i); (b) & (m); (c) & (h); (d) & (n); (e) & (k); (f) & (j); (g) & (l)
(iv) (a) row = argument; to row a boat
  (b) to bow down; a bow tie
  (c) sow = female pig; to sow seeds
  (d) tear = to cut or rip; to shed a tear
  (e) please read this carefully; I've read it
  (f) to lead a dog; a lead pencil
  (g) bass = fish; a bass voice
  (h) invalid = sick person; invalid = not valid

Exercise 15: (a) of; off (b) of; off (c) 've; off (d) off; of (e) off; of
(f) 've; of

Exercise 16: (b) A jar of honey (d) The player was off-side (e) I could have
seen him (f) Keep off the grass

Exercise 17
(a) of England = a part of England; off England = off the coast of England
(b) 10% of the price = she kept 10%; 10% off the price = she reduced the
    price by 10%
(c) of course = naturally; off course = in the wrong direction
(d) of the record = about the record; off the record = unofficially

(e) top of the saucepan = saucepan's top; top off the saucepan = remove the top

Exercise 18: (a) offspring (b) off-hand (c) off-white (d) off-peak
(e) off-licence (f) off-shore (g) offset

Exercise 19: (a) suite (b) loose (c) adopted (d) formally (e) lathe
(f) clothes (g) recent (h) dessert (i) perfect (j) accept (k) county

Exercise 20: (a) quite; quiet (b) expect; except (c) breathe; breath
(d) latter; later (e) assured; insured (f) thorough; through

Exercise 21
(a) decent = respectable; descent = a going down
(b) personal = belonging to oneself; personnel = staff
(c) access = way in; excess = too much
(d) corporation = body of people; cooperation = working together
(e) flagrant = openly scandalous; fragrant = sweet-smelling
(f) deceased = dead; diseased = having a disease
(g) respective = individual/in turn; respectful = with respect

Section Test I: 1-C; 2-B; 3-C; 4-C; 5-C; 6-A; 7-B; 8-C; 9-B; 10-C; 11-A;
12-A; 13-A; 14-C; 15-A; 16-C; 17-B; 18-A; 19-B; 20-C

Checking Exercise II
Mistakes are:- 1. CHRISTINE 2. two THES 3. EXCEPT 4. CASUAL 5. PERHAPS 6. QUIET
7. Y-O-U-R-S-E-L-F and LATER 8. PERFECT

Exercise 22: (a) amusing (b) writing (c) breathing (d) hoping
(e) using (f) arguing (g) valuing (h) lovable (i) advisable (j) changeable
(k) courageous (l) arrival (m) survival (n) noticeably (o) translator

Exercise 23: (a) shiny (b) hazy (c) foggy (d) noisy (e) sunny
(f) sandy (g) funny (h) breezy (i) crazy (j) muddy (k) icy (l) shady

Exercise 24: (a) no smoking (b) no overtaking (c) no dancing (d) no
shouting (e) no racing (f) no trespassing (g) no skating (h) no cycling

Exercise 25: (a) forehead (b) forget (c) foresight (d) forecast
(e) foreground (f) forbid (g) foreword (h) forewarn (i) forgive
(j) fortune (k) foreman (l) forefather

Exercise 26: (a) arrangement; arranging (b) advertisement; advertising
(c) development; developing (d) excitement; exciting (e) argument; arguing
(f) achievement; achieving (g) settlement; settling (h) management;
managing (i) government; governing (j) encouragement; encouraging

Exercise 27: (b) development (d) awful (g) breathing (h) shady
(i) argument

Exercise 28: (a) nineteen pounds fifty pence (b) ninety pounds fifteen
pence (c) forty pounds fourteen pence (d) four pounds ninety pence
(e) nineteen eighty-four (f) fifteen sixty-four (g) nineteen thirty-nine
(h) fourteen fifteen (i) fifth of October (j) ninth of August (k) twelfth of
July (l) nineteenth of May

Exercise 29
(a) iron ore; either/or
(b) morale = degree of confidence; moral = good or bad
(c) humane = benevolent or considerate; human = to do with mankind
(d) bye = passage to the next round of a competition without playing a
match; by = beside (eg stand by me)
(e) heroine = female hero; heroin = a drug
(f) caste = class of people, originally Indian class; cast = to throw
(g) urbane = refined, civilised; urban = concerning a town or city
(h) loathe = to hate; loath = reluctant

Exercise 30: (a) hopefully (b) generally (c) angrily (d) incidentally
(e) childishly (f) heavily (g) financially (h) really (i) suitably
(j) successfully (k) completely (l) sensibly (m) scarcely (n) necessarily
(o) physically

Exercise 31: (b) immediately (e) fortunately (h) occasionally
(k) definitely (m) busily (n) totally

Exercise 32
(i) · (a) Yours sincerely (b) Yours faithfully (c) Yours cordially (d) Yours
truly
(ii) (a) Yours faithfully (b) Yours sincerely (c) Yours faithfully (d) Yours
sincerely (e) Yours sincerely

Exercise 33: (a) peaceful (b) careful (c) skilful (d) beautiful
(e) doubtful (f) thankful (g) wilful (h) useful (i) successful (j) awful
(k) painful (l) plentiful (m) hopeful (n) tactful (o) pitiful

Exercise 34: (b) careless (e) doubtless (f) thankless (h) useless
(k) painless (m) hopeless (n) tactless (o) pitiless

Exercise 35: (a) cheerful (b) forgetful (c) tactful (d) bashful
(e) boastful (f) resentful (g) wilful (h) resourceful (i) disrespectful

Exercise 36: (a) dissolve (b) misspell (c) dissatisfaction (d) dissimilar
(e) misstatement (f) disservice (g) dissolution (h) misshapen

Exercise 37
(i) (a) non = negative (b) sub = under (c) inter = between (d) extra = additional, special (e) post = after (f) bi = two (g) mal = bad (h) pre = before (i) multi = many (j) tele = at a distance
(ii) (a) nonentity (b) subway (c) interlock (d) extravagant
(e) postpone (f) bicentenary (g) malfunction (h) predict (i) multinational
(j) telephone

Exercise 38: (a) report, repel, retract (b) deport, detract (c) export, expel, extract (d) import, impel (e) disport, dispel, distract (f) propel, protract (g) comport (rare), compel (h) transport

Exercise 39: (a) irresponsible (b) immature (c) irrational
(d) immobile (e) illogical (f) dissimilar (g) illegible (h) unnecessary
(i) immodest (j) illiterate (k) dissatisfy (l) irrelevant

Exercise 40: (a) illegal (b) immovable (c) unnatural (d) irreparable
(e) irreplaceable (f) irresistible (g) immoral (h) irreversible

Exercise 41: (a) present (b) background (c) include (d) underrate
(e) monogamy (f) post-war (g) malevolent (h) persuade (i) associate
(j) assent

Exercise 42
(a) immoral = evil; immortal = living for ever
(b) imminent = about to happen; eminent = famous
(c) immigrate = come to a country; emigrate = leave a country
(d) implicit = implied; explicit = stated

Section Test II: 1-C; 2-C: 3-A; 4-B; 5-A; 6-C; 7-C; 8-A; 9-B; 10-C; 11-C; 12-A; 13-B; 14-B; 15-A; 16-B; 17-B; 18-C; 19-C; 20-C

Checking Exercise III:
1-S; 2-D; 3-D; 4-S; 5-D; 6-S; 7-D; 8-D; 9-D; 10-D; 11-S; 12-D; 13-D; 14-S; 15-D; 16-S; 17-D; 18-D; 19-D; 20-S; 21-D; 22-S

Exercise 43: (a) possible (b) acceptable (c) profitable (d) comparable
(e) responsible (f) dependable (g) desirable (h) probable (i) visible
(j) comprehensible (k) imaginable (l) credible (m) accessible
(n) avoidable (o) agreeable

Exercise 44: (a) impossible (b) unacceptable (c) unprofitable
(d) incomparable (e) irresponsible (f) undependable (g) undesirable
(h) improbable (i) invisible (j) incomprehensible (k) unimaginable
(l) incredible (m) inaccessible (n) unavoidable (o) disagreeable

Exercise 45: (a) indelible — (iii) (b) illegible - (i) (c) inedible - (v)
(d) ineligible - (iv) (e) intelligible - (ii)

Exercise 46: (a) inconsiderable - (ix) (b) indispensable - (v) (c) inflammable
- (vii) (d) impracticable - (iv) (e) incompatible - (x) (f) invaluable - (iii)

Exercise 47: (a) absent (b) distant (c) important (d) reluctant
(e) recent (f) permanent (g) innocent (h) relevant (i) competent
(j) adjacent (k) component (l) extravagant

Exercise 48: (a) reference (b) conference (c) allowance (d) sentence
(e) influence (f) performance (g) preference (h) convenience
(i) independence (j) tolerance

Exercise 49: (a) difference (b) endurance (c) existence
(d) appearance (e) assurance (f) insurance (g) disturbance (h) residence
(i) entrance (j) offence (k) pretence (l) maintenance

Exercise 50: (a) confident (b) ignorant (c) insistent (d) resistant
(e) observant (f) pleasant (g) obedient (h) abundant (i) sufficient
(j) dominant (k) excellent (l) apparent

Exercise 51: (a) doctor (b) operator (c) prisoner (d) director
(e) burglar (f) professor (g) sponsor (h) negotiator (i) solicitor
(j) barrister

Exercise 52: (a) inventor (b) designer (c) organiser (d) surveyor
(e) inspector (f) decorator (g) editor (h) translator (i) commuter
(j) conductor (k) supervisor (l) adviser

Exercise 53: (b) computer (c) familiar (d) regular (f) grammar
(h) calculator (i) similar (k) particular

Exercise 54: (a) circular (b) nuclear (c) muscular (d) spectacular
(e) rectangular (f) solar (g) lunar (h) stellar

Exercise 55: (a) little (b) quarrel (c) people (d) technical (e) vehicle
(f) casual (g) identical (h) handle (i) medical (j) ankle (k) visual
(l) jungle (m) annual (n) physical

Exercise 56: (a) library (b) mystery (c) factory (d) ordinary
(e) compulsory (f) cemetery (g) temporary (h) secretary (i) primary
(j) memory (k) snobbery (l) summary (m) anniversary (n) honorary
(o) confectionery (p) accessory

Exercise 57: (a) oral (b) mental (c) dental (d) manual (e) vocal
(f) dorsal

Exercise 58: (a) mobile (b) model (c) mogul (d) metal (e) mettle
(f) methyl (g) menthol

Exercise 59: (a) boxes (b) dresses (c) wives (d) churches (e) taxes
(f) thieves (g) selves (h) dishes (i) knives (j) sixes (k) wishes
(l) watches

Exercise 60: (a) life (b) address (c) shelf (d) authority (e) exercise
(f) inquiry (g) sentry (h) lady (i) half (j) business

Exercise 61: (a) parties (b) monkeys (c) apologies (d) berries
(e) butterflies (f) opportunities (g) secretaries (h) jerseys (i) difficulties
(j) factories (k) valleys (l) lorries

Exercise 62: (a) chimneys (d) journeys (f) anniversaries (h) skies
(i) loaves

Exercise 63: (a) radios (b) potatoes (c) photos (d) heroes
(e) pianos (f) tomatoes (g) solos (h) vetoes

Exercie 64: (a) woman (b) tooth (c) foot (d) goose (e) deer
(f) child (g) ox (h) sheep (i) shoe (j) echo (k) toe (l) medium

Exercise 65: (a) news is (b) artists are (c) series is (d) politics is/are
(e) economics is/are (f) scissors are (g) crisis is (h) athletics is/are

Exercise 66: (b) information (c) sugar (e) equipment (g) furniture
(j) progress

Section Test III: 1-C; 2-C; 3-C; 4-A; 5-A; 6-C; 7-B; 8-B; 9-B; 10-C; 11-B;
12-C; 13-B; 14-C; 15-A; 16-A; 17-C; 18-A; 19-A; 20-C

Exercise 67: (a) advice; advise (b) licence; licensed (c) practise;
practise (d) devised; device

Exercise 68: (b) netball practice (c) out of practice (e) put into practice

Exercise 69: (a) advice (b) advised (c) device (d) practice
(e) devised (f) prophecy (g) devices (h) advise (i) Practise (j) licence
(k) advice (l) prophesied (m) licence; practise

Exercise 70: (a) beating (b) hitting (c) treating (d) cutting
(e) sitting (f) knitting (g) winning (h) meaning (i) running (j) planning

(k) groaning (l) spinning (m) sleeping (n) hopping (o) shopping
(p) leaping (q) dropping (r) drooping

Exercise 71: (a) dropped (b) heated (c) robbed (d) planned
(e) gritted (f) rubber (g) hitter (h) planner (i) reader (j) stopper
(k) breakage (l) stoppage (m) wreckage (n) haulage (o) scrummage

Exercise 72

(a) big	bigger	biggest
(b) fit	fitter	fittest
(c) cool	cooler	coolest
(d) wet	wetter	wettest
(e) dear	dearer	dearest
(f) mean	meaner	meanest
(g) sad	sadder	saddest
(h) tall	taller	tallest
(i) bad	worse	worst
(j) good	better	best

Exercise 73: (a) belief (b) field (c) conceit (d) thief (e) seize
(f) weight (g) neighbour (h) eight (i) freight (j) vein (k) hygiene
(l) protein (m) diesel (n) siege (o) receipt

Exercise 74: (a) foreign (b) view (c) friend (d) leisure (e) height
(f) weird (g) fierce (h) pierce (i) weir (j) sieve

Exercise 75: (c) believe (f) receive (g) achieve

Exercise 76: (a) perception (b) relief (c) belief (d) deceit/ deception
(e) grief (f) reception/receipt (g) achievement (h) retrieval

Exercise 77: (a) piece (b) seize (c) eight (d) weigh (e) heir
(f) reign (g) veil (h) vein

Exercise 78: (a) gnat (b) knot (c) gnaw (d) know (e) knew
(f) knight (g) pneumonia (h) gnarled (i) knuckle (j) pneumatic

Exercise 79: (a) wrist (c) wrinkle (e) wreck (reck is rare) (f) wrong
(g) wren (i) wrestle (l) wriggle

Exercise 80
(a) whether or not; fine weather
(b) car wheel; we'll go tomorrow
(c) Where is it? I'll wear it
(d) Which one? she's a witch
(e) don't whine; red wine

Exercise 81: (a) heard (b) hare (c) air (d) whole (e) hoarse (f) our
(g) hale (h) hymn

Exercise 83: (a) column (b) thumb (c) bomb (d) condemn
(e) climb (f) hymn (g) crumb (h) dumb

Exercise 84: (a) doubt (b) folk (c) debt (d) design (e) could
(f) campaign (g) palm (h) reign

Exercise 85: (a) catch (b) watch (c) wash (d) stitch (e) whistle
(f) Christmas (g) bachelor (h) committee (i) attach (j) mortgage

Exercise 86: (a) excuse (b) excellent (c) exercise (d) excitement
(e) exist (f) excess (g) acquire (h) absence (i) scissors (j) luscious
(k) obsolete (l) conscious

Exercise 87: (a) b (b) c (c) d (d) p (e) w (f) p (g) n   might be
silent (h) h (i) n (j) c

Exercise 88: l i g h t

Section Test IV: 1-A; 2-C; 3-A; 4-B; 5-A; 6-C; 7-B; 8-B; 9-A; 10-C; 11-C;
12-B; 13-C; 14-A; 15-A; 16-B; 17-C; 18-A; 19-B; 20-C

Punctuation

Exercise 89
(a) You forgot to feed the tropical fish.
(d) She danced with feeling and grace.
(f) Edinburgh is the capital city of Scotland.
(g) She slammed the food down in front of her husband.
(h) Good morning.

Exercise 90
(b) Please sit down.
(c) The ice was dangerously thin.
(g) Please don't cut too much off.
(h) He wanted to be a surgeon but he couldn't stand the sight of blood.
(i) Note-taking is a very useful skill.

Exercise 91
(a) I like this programme. It's educational.
(b) He was not very old but he was nearly bald.
(c) It has rained all week. The farmers are happy again.
(d) You can't wear that dress, Mary. It's far too tight. It's not nice.

(e) If you don't believe me, ask Ted. You know he always tells the truth.

(f) He turned over and yawned widely.

(g) Don't touch that wire. You'll electrocute yourself.

(h) They went into the club. It was quiet and almost empty. They turned round and came out into the dark streets again.

(i) With all the noise that was going on around her she found it very hard to concentrate on her work.

(j) I love him. I shall marry him if he asks me.

Exercise 92

Sarah had never been out with a boy before so this evening was the first time. She wasn't sure whether she was looking forward to it or not. She was certainly excited. She stood in front of the sitting-room fire in her new dress and tried to talk sensibly to her mother as she waited nervously for Edmund. She didn't have long to wait. She soon heard his footsteps coming up the front path. The door opened and in he came. Her heart sank. He was wearing jeans and a dirty denim jacket.

Exercise 93

(a) Will you give me a ride on your motorbike?

(b) You are earning less than you would get if you were out of work.

(c) The Principal gave an impressive speech.

(d) What is today's date?

(e) Today is August 11th.

(f) Why are you making so much noise?

(g) I can't be bothered to work in the evenings.

(h) Is it true that Ben and Alison have broken up?

(i) Your library book is long overdue.

(j) When does the disco start tonight?

Exercise 94

(a) I know why she refuses to go out with you.

(b) Why didn't you vote for me as student president?

(c) She asked if she could try on the long cotton dress.

(d) Why don't my parents leave me alone?

(e) He had no idea why she would not talk to him.

(f) I don't understand how you can support the present Government.

(g) Can you lend me some money, Bill?

(h) Whether it's raining or not, I shall still go for a walk after dinner.

(i) Does John Travolta really have blue eyes?

(j) Why didn't you ask that policeman where the station is?

Exercise 95

(a) What a good tea that was!

(b) What are we having for tea?

(c) Let me out!

(d) Tibby! Stop scratching the furniture!
(e) How unusual to meet a man who is interested in needlework!
(f) Dearest, I love you.
(g) Oh no! He's dropped it!
(h) How are we going to climb that cliff?
(i) Mum! Come here!
(j) Look out! You'll knock over that old man!
(The exclamation marks at the end of (d), (g), (i) and (j) are optional; they could be full stops. There could be an exclamation mark at the end of (f).)

Exercise 96
(a) Toby Sinclair has lived in India for three years.
(b) One of Britain's most popular television programmes was 'The Forsyte Saga'.
(c) Jane Toogood and Henry Clark were married in St Peter's Church on Saturday.
(d) He always spent his summer holiday looking at Saxon churches.
(e) The Italians are usually considered to be more emotional than the English.
(f) 'Murder on the Orient Express' was a film made from the novel by Agatha Christie.
(g) Mrs Williams took her old Austin to the village garage.
(h) You will find the offices of J W Brodie Ltd at the end of Market Street.
(i) The Royal Air Force suffered heavy losses during the Battle of Britain.
(j) I can't make up my mind whether I am a Christian, an agnostic or an atheist.

Exercise 97
(a) It would help the builders if they could have immediate delivery of the frames, glass, catches and hinges.
(b) It is just as important for a secretary to be clean, neat, punctual and polite as it is for her to be a good typist.
(c) She wondered whether he would prefer to go for a walk, watch television, read a book or just talk.
(d) Wilkie, Stonehouse, Dibley and Hazell were an effective goal-scoring combination.
(e) The firemen put out the flames quickly, quietly and efficiently.
(f) The green plover, peewit or lapwing can be identified by the round shape of its wings when in flight.
(g) He packed his toothbrush, toothpaste and pyjamas and set off for the station.
(h) The night club was crowded, smoky, dark and noisy.
(i) She would not go out with any of them — Dave, Jack, Pete, Harry or even Sylvester.
(j) He did not know whether to put on his brakes, swerve violently or just go straight on and hope for the best.

Exercise 98

(a) The tyres, squealing as they went round the corner, were beginning to show signs of wear.

(b) My grandfather, a well-known citizen of the town, had a street named after him.

(c) Sid Green, who had done no work that morning, was told off by the foreman.

(d) John made no attempt to speak to Carol, who was sulking in front of the television.

(e) Shouting at the tops of their voices, the crowd cheered the home team to victory.

(f) This morning I met Jack Banks, of whom you spoke yesterday.

(g) The cat licked its fur, singed by the sparks from the fire.

(h) The uneven wicket, because of which many balls bounced viciously, was responsible for the dismissal of the first four batsmen.

(i) The new stand, recently built by the contractors, was a great success.

(j) The Fastnet yacht race claimed several casualties, mostly from the smaller boats.

Exercise 99

(a) I loved the blouse which you were wearing yesterday.

(b) Sally saw Mr Chapman, the manager of the supermarket, for a preliminary interview.

(c) Eddy, who had never fished before, caught three mackerel off the rocks with a spinner.

(d) Holding each other closely as they danced, they were oblivious of all around them.

(e) The man who is wearing the brown jacket is the man who tried to pick my pocket.

(f) She was pleased to give a pound to the charity for which the children were collecting.

(g) A large cheque was sent to Oxfam, on behalf of which the children were collecting.

(h) Gordon Lee's recent release, 'Troubled', has wasted no time in getting to the top of the charts.

(i) They leaned over the rails and watched the horses parading round the paddock.

(j) The programme, 'Killer', which was on the television last night, was very frightening.

Exercise 100

(a) Tom knew he would have to work really hard if he was going to pass his exams.

(b) Although you have the qualities we need, I am afraid we do not have a vacancy.

(c) The family agreed that, while Tessa was studying, they would not have the radio on.

(d) They agreed that they would not have the radio on while Tessa was studying.

(e) The match will not be played unless the pitch dries out.

(f) She said that, because he had lied to her, she could never trust him again.

(g) When Bonzo was six months old, his training began.

(h) The English, although they had a smaller army, defeated the French because they were better armed.

(i) After they had put the ferrets in, the boys waited hopefully for rabbits to come out into the nets.

(j) She was furious with Marcel because he had dyed her hair the wrong colour.

Exercise 101

(a) Good afternoon, Mrs Arbuthnot.

(b) Ladies and gentlemen, this is a great occasion.

(c) I must ask you, Mr Wiggins, to accept my resignation.

(d) Get off my foot, you fat lump.

(e) Sarah, will you lend me that record you bought last week?

(f) If you do not move further up the beach, Your Majesty, I fear you will get your feet wet.

(g) Platoon, attention!

(h) You rotten thing, you've taken my queen.

(i) The most important thing to remember, Daisy, is that the customer is always right.

(j) Why did you steal that pig, Tom?

Exercise 102

(a) "My punctuation is improving," she said hopefully.

(b) He began briskly, "Today we shall learn about cyclones and their effects."

(c) "Why won't you come out with me?" he asked desperately.

(d) Swaying over the microphone, the DJ said smoothly, "It's great to see you all this evening."

(e) "If you had shown some common sense, the accident would never have occurred," he said sternly.

(f) "Look out!" yelled the foreman.

(g) Mary asked nervously, "Is the meal all right?"

(h) "Help!" the man in the hang-glider shouted down from above their heads.

(i) "I still haven't found a job," she said sadly.

(j) The zoo-keeper said, "Move slowly or you'll frighten him."

Exercise 103

(a) The rescuers, however, held out little hope of finding the man alive.

(b) Of course the vandals had to pay for repairing the damage.

(c) The vandals had, of course, to pay for repairing the damage.

(d) Well, there was nothing we could do about it.

(e) It was, moreover, a particularly windy evening.

(f) We were pleased to see him nevertheless.

(g) By the way, have you met Jane Simpson?

(h) You are, without doubt, the biggest liar I have ever met.

(i) However, they did not play the music as loudly as we had feared.

(j) The ball, meanwhile, had gone out of play.

(It would be possible to write a comma after *of course* in (b). The commas could be left out in (c), (h) and (j). The answers given above, however, are probably the most suitable.)

Exercise 104

(a) "I'm sorry," he apologised.

(b) Dan suggested, "Let's stop at the next pub."

(c) "Don't leave me!" she sobbed.

(d) "Why don't you look where you're going?" demanded the old man as he struggled up from the pavement.

(e) "I nearly caught it," said John as the fish wriggled off the hook and slipped back into the water.

(f) "This election has been rigged!" cried the losing candidate.

(g) Mrs Baker said sadly, "My pot plants always die."

(h) "I hope you're sorry for all the trouble you've caused," said the magistrate sternly.

(i) "Two coffees, please," said Jenny.

(j) Sleepily she asked, "What time is it?"

Exercise 105

(a) "This pen always runs out of ink at the wrong time," muttered Charles to himself.

(b) The Prime Minister said that she would have no arguments in her Cabinet.

(c) The sergeant told his men, "Don't shoot until you see the whites of their eyes!"

(d) "What is the name of this station?" he asked, stretching himself and looking sleepily out of the carriage window.

(e) "We've won!" they shouted.

(f) Mrs Tappit asked her class how they expected to become typists without being able to spell correctly.

(g) He held the dead ferret in his hand and said sadly, "I'll miss Fred — he was the best I've ever had."

(h) "Can I borrow your hair-drier, please, Mum?" asked Karen.

(i) "You will kill yourself if you go on smoking," advised Dr Williams.

(j) Dr Williams told him that he would kill himself if he went on smoking.

Exercise 106

(a) "Dinner will be served during the flight," the air hostess told the passengers.

(b) "Can you really concentrate on your work with the radio on so loudly?" Harry's mother asked.

(c) "Nobody will give you a job," said the careers officer, "unless you cut your nails and comb your hair."

(d) He said firmly, "I'm not going to play cards with you again."

(e) "Do you really think you look attractive," asked Aunt Helen, "walking around with dirty jeans and holes in your tee-shirt?"

(f) "These trousers are far too tight," Mark told the sales assistant.

(g) "I'm very impressed," said the manager, "and I should like to offer you the job."

(h) "Eureka!" cried Archimedes.

(i) "You were unwise," said Mrs Jenks, "to paint the walls blue and the ceiling orange."

(j) "Bonzo!" shouted his master. "Come here at once!"

Exercise 107

"Hello," said the boy who had just appeared in front of her.

"Hello," said Penny. He was obviously nervous so she smiled at him.

"Would you like a drink?" he asked.

"No thanks," she said. "Would you like to sit down?" He sat down in the empty chair beside her and for a moment they looked in silence at the couples dancing in front of them.

"Have you come by yourself?" he asked. Penny hesitated. She didn't know whether to tell him that she had had an argument with Barry and that he'd gone off by himself.

"No," she said, "but I'm by myself now. What about you?"

"I'm by myself," he said. "My name's Stephen." He hesitated then he looked at her and smiled for the first time. "Shall we dance?"

"Yes," she said, "let's dance."

Exercise 108

(a) The train's whistle	(k) The ladies' room
(b) The pattering raindrops	(l) At the doctor's
(c) The hitch-hikers' rucksacks	(m) The sandwiches on the plate
(d) A bunch of bananas	(n) A day's illness
(e) The rustling leaves	(o) The donkeys on the beach
(f) The rabbits' burrows	(p) A bus-load of holiday-makers
(g) The clouds passing overhead	(q) The cheering spectators
(h) The firemen's helmets	(r) The chimpanzees' tea-party
(i) Mary's little lamb	(s) For heaven's sake
(j) The bustling crowd of shoppers	(t) The rose bushes

Exercise 109

(a) The book's cover

(b) The men's leader

(c) My brother's girl-friend

(d) The Hikers' Association

(e) Journey's end

(f) The ladies' netball team

(g) The ship's crew

(h) A month's notice

(i) The Transport and General Workers' Union

(j) A smoker's cough

Exercise 110

(a) 'The Times' has been one of the country's leading newspapers for about two hunderd years.

(b) Dickson's savage shot bounced dangerously out of the goal-keeper's hands.

(c) 'Gardeners' Question-Time' is one of the longest-running radio programmes.

(d) Heather and Fiona bought two pieces of cod and two bags of chips.

(e) The Women's Lib movement has a large number of supporters in this country, rather more in the towns and cities than in the villages.

(f) The students' eyes were firmly fixed on Mr Metcalfe as he spoke sternly from the platform, nor did the Principal's words fall on deaf ears.

(g) The clown's trousers were baggy and full of holes.

(h) The parables of Jesus have at times been misunderstood.

(i) Edinburgh, Scotland's capital, is one of the world's beautiful cities.

(j) Bill Jones's overalls were lost so he bought some new ones.

Exercise 111

(a) I'll see if there's any cake left in the tin.

(b) We shan't get there in time if you don't hurry.

(c) The dog won't go outside if it's raining.

(d) It's not fair — you're cheating.

(e) The light's gone out and I can't find the candles.

(f) Let's go and see if Sally's home yet.

(g) It's a nuisance but there's no use worrying about it now.

(h) If he's not home by ten o'clock, I'll lock the front door.

(i) You'll be sorry for what you've done when your father's finished with you.

(j) I'm afraid I've dropped a mug and it's lost its handle.

Exercise 112

(a) Desmond and Diana thought the film was very bad; they decided to leave.

(b) Sally rushed breathlessly into the office; she was late for work again.

(c) The motor-cyclist lay on the road, his right leg twisted at an impossible angle.

(d) The motor-cyclist lay on the road; his right leg was twisted at an impossible angle.

(e) Father came in from the garden; it was getting dark.

(f) The family were all watching the play on the television. Dick suddenly leapt to his feet.
(g) Miss Wilkinson put on her coat; it had started to rain.
(h) She lay in bed, sleeping peacefully until late in the morning.
(i) Wendy was tall and had beautiful black hair; her sister was short and fair.
(j) James lifted his eyes from his exam paper and looked out of the window. On the other side of the road he could see children playing in the park.

Exercise 113

(a) There were four things which old Mr Bassett disliked: long hair, loud whistling, hands in pockets and mumbled speech.
(b) This was the rallying-cry of the French Revolution: "Liberty, Equality, Fraternity."
(c) The walls of Jenny's bedroom were completely covered with a colourful collection of various things: photos, pictures, posters, record jackets and other odds and ends.
(d) There were two reasons why Sebastian Ellis never went to parties: his dislike of crowds and his enjoyment of work.
(e) The spy knew there was only one thing he could do now: swallow his suicide pill so that he could tell nothing to his captors.
(f) What Jerry really liked about college was this: the chance to be responsible for himself.
(g) The pools-winner's shopping-list was simple but expensive: a large house, a smart car and a complete wardrobe of new clothes.
(h) These were his last words: "I leave everything to you."
(i) Tom's favourite meal was breakfast and his favourite breakfast was always the same: grapefruit, boiled egg, toast and coffee.
(j) The prisoners-of-war felt they had one main duty: to escape.

Exercise 114

(a) The VC (Victoria Cross) was instituted in 1856 and is awarded for conspicuous bravery.
(b) The writer argues strongly (chapter 3) that larger organisations are usually less efficient than smaller ones.
(c) For almost twenty years Sir Leonard Hutton held the record (364) for the highest score ever made in a Test Match.
(d) Her birthday (1st January) always made it easy to calculate her age.
(e) Tickets (£1.50 and £1) may be bought at the door.
(f) Please telephone the Fixtures Secretary (Langdon 2784) if you need to find out whether a match has been cancelled.
(g) The moa (illustration on page 72) was the largest of the flightless birds found in New Zealand.
(h) The exclamation mark (!) should be used sparingly.
(i) The City Library (15 High Street) has an excellent reference section.
(j) The kilogram (2.2 lbs) is at last beginning to be accepted by British housewives.

Exercise 115

(a) The highest shade temperature recorded in Britain was 38°C (100.5°F) in Kent in 1868.

(b) The two comics, Thunder and Lightning (Lightning is the thin one), made the audience laugh uproariously.

(c) The cuckoo has arrived (have you heard one yet?) so it must be spring.

(d) To cross the bridge over the Avon motorists are required to pay a toll (5p).

(e) Adrian didn't recognise Mrs Webster (she had dyed her hair blonde) until she told him who she was.

(f) Mrs Tasker could not attend her daughter's wedding (what a dreadful shame!) because she was in hospital.

(g) The first successful gramophone was constructed by Thomas Alva Edison (1847-1931).

(h) I wasn't sorry when Simon (silly fool!) fell in the river.

(i) The population of Albania is 2 616 000 (1977 estimate).

(j) For next week's party I need a pair of black boots, a bow tie (can you lend me yours?), some pin-striped trousers and a bowler hat.

Exercise 116

(a) She looked down at the broken cup — why was she so careless? — and went to get a cloth.

(b) The exhausted racing pigeon — he thought it must be one of Mr Weston's — sat motionless on the grass.

(c) Jack looked quickly over his shoulder — had the policeman seen him? — and concentrated on walking calmly down the road.

(d) Alfie Sykes — what a clumsy oaf! — had trodden on the sandwiches again.

(e) The men went back to work — they had finally accepted the management's pay offer — and the factory resumed full production.

(f) Terry looked carefully at the girl by the window — had he seen her before? — and decided to go across and talk to her.

(g) Simon looked at his watch — how late Jane always was! — and pulled his coat more tightly about him.

(h) The family emerged wearily from the shelter — the all-clear had sounded — and went slowly back into the house.

(i) During the night — what a violent storm! — I hardly slept.

(j) That dress — I'm sorry to be rude — just does not suit you.

Exercise 117

(a) Eleanor has one good quality above all — she's always cheerful.

(b) "Let's put that poster behind the door — no, over the table — no, this is the best place."

(c) The mysterious meat-thief, caught in the act, stood there quite unashamed — the next-door dog.

(d) She lay on her back at the top of the cliff and listened to the sound that always reminded her of her childhood — the calling of the gulls.

(e) "The goal-keeper's saved it − no, he's dropped it − it's a goal!"
(f) He was sorry but the price of the ring was just too high − over fifty pounds.
(g) "I'll tell you why we've got so few customers today − there's a bus strike."
(h) "I'd like a pizza, please − no, I'll change that to a steak − no, I think I'll have spaghetti instead, thank you."
(i) "Let's cross the road now − no, wait − right, let's go."
(j) To be successful there's something you need more than brains − hard work.

Exercise 118

(a)	cro-cus	(f)	cup-board	(k)	win-dow	(p)	month-ly
(b)	rose	(g)	ward-robe	(l)	mach-ine	(q)	rul-er
(c)	pen-cil	(h)	car-pet	(m)	door	(r)	kick-ed
(d)	pen	(i)	cur-tain	(n)	week-ly	(s)	splash-ing
(e)	pa-pers	(j)	rug	(o)	fort-night	(t)	div-ing

Exercise 119
(a) Wearily he bent down to tie his shoe-laces.
(b) A red-hot coal tumbled from the fire and lay smouldering on the carpet.
(c) The villain of the film was a baby-faced gangster called Sylvester.
(d) The ancient stones reared towards the sky in an impressive semi-circle.
(e) The moist atmosphere condensed on the window-panes and ran down in untidy streams.
(f) Anna was always bright-eyed and fresh-faced.
(g) Forget-me-nots were Susie's favourite flowers.
(h) As usual, Mr Bellinger set off for home with a bulging brief-case.
(i) The Kavanaghs lived in the pleasant Wiltshire town of Bradford-on-Avon.
(j) "You're a two-faced, double-crossing horn-swoggler!" cried Hank angrily.

Common errors

Exercise 120
(a) = I was the only person who wanted to see Mr Spencer
(b) = it was the only thing I wanted to do
(c) = Mr Spencer was the only person I wanted to see
(d) = all I wanted to talk about was my son
(e) = I have only one son
Note that in each case *only* refers to the word which immediately follows it.

Exercise 121
(a) He badly wanted to play the guitar.
(b) Chambermaid required until September. Must be respectable.

(c) My uncle, in his pyjamas, shot the elephant.
(d) Piano with carved legs for sale by lady.
(e) He saw the silver necklace hanging round her neck.
(f) Still wearing a dressing gown, she paid the milkman.
(g) Room, 20 foot by 15 foot, to let. Suitable for young person.
(h) Headache? Let us examine your eyes and remove it.
(i) When you are flying in the air, houses look funny.
(j) On the expedition I myself hunted and shot.
(k) Sports car with MOT wanted by young man.

Exercise 122
(a) already (b) all ready (c) already (d) always (e) all ways
(f) always (g) always (h) all together (i) altogether (j) altogether (k) all
together (l) may be (m) Maybe (n) into (o) in to (p) into (q) no
body (r) nobody (s) Sometimes (t) some times

Exercise 123
(a) herself (c) cannot (e) Thank you (f) a lot (h) together (j) could
not (k) tonight (l) all right (m) on to

Exercise 124: (a) took (b) taken (c) taken (d) took (e) rung
(f) rang (g) rung (h) rang (i) seen (j) drove (k) swum (l) torn

Exercise 125
(a) You shouldn't have spoken to him like that.
(c) You might have shown more sympathy.
(d) When she ran out of the room, she tore her dress.
(e) It had just begun to snow.
(f) They went to Spain and drank too much.
(g) Last week our team was beaten 2-0.

Exercise 126: (a) Lie (b) Lay (c) lay (d) lie (e) lay (f) lie

Exercise 127: (a) rise (b) raise (c) rise (d) raise (e) raise (f) rise

Exercise 128
(a) She was laid low by flu.
(b) The river has already risen two feet.
(e) The temperature had risen 20 degrees.
(f) She hung the washing in the garden.
(i) We raised an objection to the plan.

Exercise 129: (a) of (b) from (c) (no preposition) (d) on (e) from
(f) with (g) from (h) (no preposition)

Exercise 130: (a) to (b) of (c) of (d) to (e) as to (f) at (g) of
(h) with (i) of (j) as to

Exercise 131
(a) Subject. He and I paid the bill.
(b) Object. The bill was paid by him.
(c) Subject. Susan and he are going together.
(d) Subject. He spilled the soup.
(e) Object. Nobody was late except him.

Exercise 132
(a) Did you hear about Jill and me?
(b) She met me at the station.
(c) Then Jill and I went to a party.
(d) She and I had an argument.
(e) Jill said I was to blame.
(f) As for me, I thought it was her fault.
(g) It never occurred to me that I was wrong.
(h) She said she never wanted to see the likes of me again.
(i) I don't know what's going to happen to Jill and me.

Exercise 133
(b) I am proud of you and him.
(d) I'm going to the concert with Dan and her.
(e) You and I can take care of that.
(f) It's a matter between them and us.
(g) They gave my friend and me some good advice.
(h) Tom and I fixed the car.
(j) That's the person with whom I had the argument.
(l) They invited Jim and me to dinner.

Exercise 134
(a) Both of them are prepared to go.

(b) One of them is prepared to go.
(c) Each of them is prepared to go.
(d) Several of them are prepared to go.
(e) Many of them are prepared to go.
(f) Every one of them is prepared to go.
(g) A few of them are prepared to go.
(h) None of them is/are prepared to go.

Exercise 135
(a) Each of these examples includes a number of mistakes.
(b) Both of the men came with their tools.
(d) If anyone is looking for his books, I've got them.
(e) Each one is expected to do his best.
(h) Both she and her sister have passed their test.
(i) Everyone could make himself heard.

Exercise 136
(a) One single and one double room were available.
(c) The timetable for flights to Spain appears in our latest brochure.
(d) Most purchases in a supermarket are made on impulse.
(h) The family are all well and send their best wishes.

Exercise 137
There are many possible answers; here are some suggestions.
(a) John thought Martin was useless and told him so.
(b) Mary asked if it was June's fault.
(c) Craig told his friend, "It's your turn to pay."
(d) Tom's father is a millionaire and this makes Tom very pleased with himself.
(e) Sue felt she could never love Humphrey and told her sister so.
(f) Although the match between the staff and students was close, the former deserved to win.
(g) Before leaving, Gail had an argument with Sally.
(h) Ray went to see Jim and rode his own Yamaha.
(i) Pat thought her cousin was making a big mistake and decided to tell her.
(j) Because I learned French as a child, I can now speak it as fluently as Spanish.

Layout

Exercise 139

This would be a possible layout:

SUGGESTED IMPROVEMENTS TO
THE COLLEGE TIMETABLE

1. THE ORIGINS OF THE PRESENT TIMETABLE

2. DISADVANTAGES OF THE PRESENT TIMETABLE

    (a) Long periods of free time

    (b) Clashes of some subjects

        (i) Audio-typing and English

        (ii) Audio-typing and French

        (iii) Engineering Drawing and English

    (c) Inflexibility

3. A POSSIBLE NEW TIMETABLE

4. A SUGGESTED SCHEDULE FOR INTRODUCING A NEW TIMETABLE

    (a) Immediate action

    (b) Longer-term planning

Exercise 140

29 Western Avenue
Kilham
Lancs

14 December 1981

The Manager
Kilham Catering Ltd
Trading Estate
Kilham
Lancs

Dear Sir

You undertook to supply refreshments for approximately 1500 spectators last Saturday 12 December. There were, in fact, just under 1000 spectators but there was sufficient food and drink for only about 500.

I should be grateful if you would telephone me at Kilham 5312 to discuss the matter.

Yours faithfully

P Lenham
Hon Sec
Kilham Football Club

Exercise 141

Stanton College,
Stanton.

Tuesday, 3rd March.

Dear Mr Brotherton,

I am writing on behalf of the College Social Committee to apologise for the disturbance caused by the disco last Wednesday. Until you telephoned the Principal, we had no idea that we had made so much noise and we apologise most sincerely. It will not happen again.

I hope we shall see you at next week's meeting of the Drama Club as usual.

Yours sincerely,

Peter Mullis

Hon Sec, Stanton College Social Committee

Exercise 142

"Would you like an ice-cream?" John asked as the lights went up for the interval.

"No thanks," said Pat. "Would you?"

"No, I don't want one either. In fact, I'd like to go," said John.

"Why?" asked Pat. "Aren't you enjoying this film?"

"I'm afraid not," said John. "I think it's badly acted and unnecessarily violent. I'm not enjoying it at all."

There was a pause before Pat said, "Well, I think I agree with you." She reached under the seat for her bag and got to her feet. "Let's go then, John. It's a bit of a waste of money but there's no point sitting here not enjoying ourselves."

John smiled at her. "Thank you," he said. .